PRESIDENT
OF
PANDEMONIUM

LUKE G. WILLIAMS

PRESIDENT *of* PANDEMONIUM

THE MAD WORLD OF IKE IBEABUCHI

HAMILCAR NOIR

HARD-HITTING TRUE CRIME

ISBN: 978-1949590-35-7

Publisher's Cataloging-in-Publication Data
Names: Williams, Luke G., author.
Title: President of pandemonium : the mad world of Ike Ibeabuchi / Luke G. Williams.
Series: Hamilcar Noir
Description: Includes bibliographical references. | Boston, MA: Hamilcar Publications, 2021.
Identifiers: LCCN: 2021941134 | ISBN: 9781949590357
Subjects: LCSH Ibeabuchi, Ike. | Boxers (Sports)—Biography. | Boxers (Sports)—Nigeria. | Murder. | BISAC SPORTS & RECREATION / Boxing | BIOGRAPHY & AUTOBIOGRAPHY / Sports | TRUE CRIME / Murder / General
Classification: LCC GV1132.I24 W55 2021 | DDC 796.83/092—dc23

Hamilcar Publications
An imprint of Hannibal Boxing Media
Ten Post Office Square, 8th Floor South
Boston, MA 02109
www.hamilcarpubs.com

On the cover: Ike Ibeabuchi poses for a portrait for The Ring *in New York City in 1999.*

Frontispiece: Bad motherfucker.

For Glyn Leach

Something that is going too fast will not last until nightfall.
—Igbo proverb

The Pistor Killer

Tales of mighty strongmen and fearsome warriors are handed down proudly through the generations in Isuochi, Abia, in southeast Nigeria. Fathers tell their sons these tales—as they had been told them by their fathers—and the sons sit rapt and wide-eyed, their mouths gaping and their imaginations running wild.

Physical strength and power are seen as a birthright in this part of western Africa. It is said that Isuochi was founded by a great warrior and wrestler named Ochi, who arrived mysteriously from the east in search of a "healthy, stoneless, and windswept" landscape where he could host wrestling contests. After vanquishing all comers from a local village, Ochi never left. Many powerful men sprung from his bloodline and followed in his forbidding footsteps.

Among them was a legend known as the "Pistor Killer," whose exploits are still recounted with reverence and awe. He could carry four men hanging from his arms and on his body for more than five minutes without trembling. He could pile twelve 100-pound bags of cement on his stomach without flinching. He pulled cars with his hair, which he fashioned into a single, conical braid that made him look like an African Samson crossed with a rhinoceros.

Young children would pay two naira to watch the Pistor Killer perform his incredible feats in schoolyards, playgrounds, and gymnasiums, cheering as he defeated moving cars in tug-of-war contests, lifted 200 pounds of wood with his hair, and then reveled in the respect he engendered. Those who had been around long enough to know about such things would nod and tell the famous story of how in the 1960s the Pistor Killer had beat the legendary Kill-We Nwachukwu in a physical contest. He had even—allegedly—held Nwachukwu in the air with one hand for more than twenty seconds.

The legend of the Pistor Killer spread beyond Nigeria. In 1967, Gary Edwards, a young American who was traveling across Europe before serving as a Marine in Vietnam, recalled encountering the Pistor Killer and his manager on a train traveling from Toulon to Marseille.

"They came into our little booth on the train," Edwards said. "They were both in suits and sat down. He looked very weird, the black guy, the Pistor Killer, there was a cone of hair coming down the front of his head and sticking out. We started talking to his manager, who looked like an Italian. He showed me this scrapbook and there were all these crazy photos of the Pistor Killer. A whole bunch of pictures. Pictures of him lifting people up, pulling against fifteen or so people on the other end of a rope and picking up these amazing weights with his hair. I was thinking, *This can't be real.* I never knew someone could be that strong. And he just sat there, the Pistor Killer. He didn't speak at all."

Today a statue commemorates this folk hero, who was also known as "The Lion of Isuochi" or "Superman," but whose real name was Ibeabuchi.

And what of his descendants?

The Pistor Killer had several sons, one of whom did indeed assume his birthright. The legacy of that son—Ikemefula Charles "Ike" Ibeabuchi—is more complex and troubling, however, than that of his celebrated father.

"Before Day Turns to Dusk"

When I spoke to Ike Ibeabuchi on a February afternoon in 2016, he could scarcely believe he was free.

Maybe he knew it couldn't last. Or maybe he had become too hardened by his tour of federal institutions. Being removed from a place inhabited by killers and rapists and placed in suburbia must be disorientating. Out of the harsh and dehumanizing experience of an ICE detention center, or the sterile menace of a maximum-security prison, Ibeabuchi could now enjoy the unbroken sight of winter sunshine and the soft breeze blowing in from the desert.

As we spoke, the forty-three-year-old former heavyweight contender from Nigeria sat in a spare room of an aunt's house in Gilbert, Arizona. Because "aunt" is an appellation applied loosely in Nigeria to both blood relatives and others, it wasn't clear what Ike's connection to his "aunt" was. Regardless, since his release from custody, he had sat here for hours fixated on the world heavyweight championship he still believed was his destiny, despite the fact it was nearly seventeen years since he had thrown a punch in a prizefight. Since 1999 Ibeabuchi's professional record had stood, perfect and unbroken.

Twenty fights, twenty wins, fifteen knockouts.

When he wasn't at his aunt's, Ibeabuchi was training hard at a 24-hour branch of LA Fitness, anonymously going about the grim business of working his forty-something body into shape among insomniac gym freaks and overweight office workers. As he fielded messages on his cell phone from promotional and media bloodsuckers and posed for grainy photographs in boxing gear—snarl still on his bearded face—it must have been easy to convince himself that he still had a shot at the heavyweight title.

Images of post-prison Ibeabuchi soon began to spread across the internet, exciting those old enough to remember his thrilling war with David Tua and his shocking destruction of Chris Byrd. Social media platforms were soon ablaze with debates about whether Ibeabuchi could or should make a comeback.

Ike was happy to stoke the anticipation.

"I have unfinished business in boxing," Ibeabuchi told me, his quiet voice never wavering. "It's more a case of why shouldn't I come back, rather than why I should. My strength is that I have not been defeated. So let's fight and let's see if any heavyweights can prove or disprove my ability. Most people might think I should have retired by now, but I haven't been a world champion. To me that is an insult, so I have to redeem myself. I want to be a world champion before day turns to dusk."

Amid this optimistic defiance, however, one question got a somewhat different reaction.

"How does it feel to be free, Mr. Ibeabuchi?" I asked.

"I don't know if I am free yet," he said. "I won't feel free until I step into the ring."

Steak Knife in the Table

Most people who worked in boxing in the 1990s have an Ike Ibeabuchi story. And each one is more unbelievable than the next. One night, Ibeabuchi was having lunch in New York with his promoter Cedric Kushner and HBO executive Lou DiBella. What happened next was both bizarre and unsettling. "I can deal with anybody and I don't get scared easily," DiBella recalled. "I've seen everything in thirty years of boxing, but I never saw anyone plunge a steak knife into a table in front of me before Ike Ibeabuchi did."

DiBella continued: "We hadn't even got into serious conversation. It was just chitchat, pleasantries. I asked him: 'Where do you live, Ike?' He looked at me and said: 'Why do you want to know where I live? Why are people concerned with where I live? Is someone looking for me? Why do you want to know where I live?' And after that little expression of dismay, he plunged the fucking steak knife into the table."

Recalling the incident a year or two later, Kushner admitted that his fighter's behavior "wasn't the type of conduct I expected to romance the guy from HBO."

More than two decades later, Ibeabuchi remains an enigma. Many who knew him insist he was mentally ill to the extent that he was a danger to himself and to others. Eric Bottjer, former matchmaker for Kushner, insisted: "I've been around boxing a long time, long enough to realize that it's not a normal profession and a lot of boxers are not normal human beings, but Ike is the only fighter I've ever met who I would say was literally insane."

The legal wreckage Ibeabuchi caused from 1997 onward—including allegations, charges, or convictions connected to sexual assault, kidnapping, and attempted murder—make for grim reading, especially when you consider the human cost of his deeds, which include a teenage boy left permanently damaged and unable to walk properly as well as several prostitutes who lost their minds.

"I recall having a conversation with Cedric where I said I thought Ike was a dangerous human being who was capable of killing somebody," Bottjer recalled. "Not that he had made any threats to me or anybody on our staff, but, being around him, that was the impression I formed. Thankfully he never did [murder anyone] but having said that he certainly did harm to that boy in Texas and the woman in Las Vegas."

There's another narrative, however, advanced by Ike himself and his late mother Patricia—a tale of conspiracy in which mysterious men stole embryos to breed a future world heavyweight champion. It's the type of story you might find in the pages of a pulp novel, one in which Ibeabuchi is the victim, a man immersed in the corrupt world of boxing who encounters exploitation at every turn. There are also those who firmly deny Ibeabuchi is the crazed monster he has often been portrayed as. "Ike was a good man with a good heart," insists Bill Benton, the trainer and matchmaker who was arguably closer to him than anyone else in the boxing business. "Forget boxing, he did beautiful and good things that people never talk about."

Putting aside for now Ibeabuchi's mental health, we must first look at what can't be questioned, the facts of his boxing career—facts that have helped him reach mythical status in heavyweight boxing history. His record—20-0 with 15 knockouts—isn't necessarily impressive. In modern boxing any mediocre heavyweight who is guided carefully can build such a record. What created Ibeabuchi's status as one of boxing's great "what if" stories were two defining fights—the ones he fought against David Tua in 1997 and Chris Byrd in 1999.

The strength of these two performances as well as images of Ibeabuchi exchanging bombs with Tua and knocking out Byrd—conjure what might have happened had he battled the likes of Lennox Lewis, Evander Holyfield, and Mike Tyson.

Boxing fans love to debate what could have been, particularly when it comes to wasted or unfulfilled talent. Ike, however, doesn't give a fuck: "The Holyfield fight did not happen, nor Lewis or Tyson," he declared. "Commenting on them would be crying over spilled milk."

"Mere Anarchy Is Loosed Upon the World"

"**N**igeria," said writer and statesman Obafemi Awolowo, "is not a nation . . . it is a mere geographical expression. There are no 'Nigerians' in the same sense as there are 'English,' 'Welsh,' or 'French.' The word 'Nigerian' is merely a distinctive appellation to distinguish those who live within the boundaries of Nigeria and those who do not."

Nigeria's sense of national identity has evolved rapidly since Awolowo's words in 1947. Nevertheless, the Nigeria that Ike Ibeabuchi was born into on February 2, 1973, was fraught with political, ethnic, and religious divisions and tensions—which was a legacy of the brutal thoughtlessness of colonialism (when Africans from hundreds of different ethnic groups were placed under European rule into arbitrarily determined administrative regions).

After Nigeria gained independence in 1960, a civil war raged between 1967 and 1970, ending with the defeat and reintegration of Biafra, a secessionist state in the southeast. Biafra reflected an effort by the Igbo people, one of the largest ethnic groups in Nigeria, to establish an independent nation. The failure of the Biafran dream came with an awful cost, and it was estimated that one to three million people died from war and famine.

The Ibeabuchis are Igbo, but how much the events of the 1970s affected Ike is unclear. Published interviews tend to skirt over his youth, although some insights have emerged. "I didn't grow up in Nigeria," Ibeabuchi told Joe Santoliquito of *KO* magazine in 1999. "I thought I did, but I grew up here [in the United States]. I was nineteen when I came to the United States but I feel grown right now, and what I know now I didn't know then in Nigeria. So that's growing up to me. . . . It was okay in Nigeria. It's not an easy country at all . . . it's not like here. It's ruled by the military."

Igbo areas of Nigeria suffered hardship during the 1970s, as much infrastructure got destroyed during the war. Rebuilding happened slowly, and wasn't helped by what many saw as institutional and vindictive bias against the Igbo in government departments.

The complex gender politics of Igbo culture, which emphasized and idolized masculine ideals, also can't be underestimated when looking at Ibeabuchi's personality. Such concepts are explored brilliantly in Chinua Achebe's classic 1958 novel *Things Fall Apart*, and there are multiple parallels between the rise and fall of Achebe's fictional protagonist Okonkwo and Ike Ibeabuchi. Like Ibeabuchi, who rose to stardom with a famous triumph against Tua, Okonkwo gains prominence through a memorable wrestling match against "Amalinze the Cat." As the novel progresses, however, a chain of calamitous events causes a dramatic fall from grace that involves exile and eventual suicide—a sad fall that reflects Ibeabuchi's own descent. Okonkwo's ever-present fear of failure ultimately determines his fate. With his ferocity, pride, and impulsivity, Okonkwo serves not only as a symbol of Igbo masculinity, but also speaks to the wider flaws of man, separate from nationality or ethnicity. The title of Achebe's novel, an allusion to W. B. Yeats's poem "The Second Coming," serves as a sad metaphor for Ibeabuchi's career, which once looked bound for limitless heights but self-destructed in a blaze of madness:

Things fall apart; the centre cannot hold;
Mere anarchy is loosed upon the world,
The blood-dimmed tide is loosed, and everywhere
The ceremony of innocence is drowned . . .

It was hard for Ibeabuchi growing up in a culture where you always had to prove yourself to "be a man"—something that would of course have been reinforced by his father's folk-hero status. Because of his father's work, Ike's family also moved around a lot for several years, including two years in Ghana, where he attended kindergarten.

Strangely, Ibeabuchi has only publicly touched on his father's influence briefly. Before his professional boxing debut in October 1994, he proudly told the Shreveport, Louisiana, *Times* of his father's achievements, insisting that "I inherit my strength from him." By 1999, however, in conversation with *KO*, Ibeabuchi's attitude toward his father seemed more ambivalent. "We're both strong mentally and physically. My dad was just like me growing up. He boxed a little but he was a showman. He did the circus strongman things, lifting stuff. That's not where I get my gift from. This thing here is more natural. What I have is more mental."

Another powerful force in Ibeabuchi's life was religion. He was raised a devout Christian, the faith that—in another indication of colonialism's transformative influence—permeated the Igbo through the nineteenth and twentieth centuries. His late mother Patricia once said that "as a preacher of God's Word, I raised Ike and my other children to know what God's word says and that we are to live our lives according to the Word of God." It is a faith that has endured for Ibeabuchi's whole life. When interviewed by *The Ring*, in November 1997, he declared: "I'm on a mission from God. . . . Boxing is just part of my mission." Additionally, his short-lived personal website carried the slogan "God First," which was also emblazoned on the waistband of his trunks and robe for several of his pro fights.

Once his family returned to Nigeria from Ghana, Ibeabuchi enrolled at the Housing Estate Primary School Aladinma Owerri, a state school where his athletic abilities developed through a love of soccer and wrestling. At his high school, Emmanuel College Owerri, Ibeabuchi did well academically, majoring in sciences and developing the ambition to be a doctor. He hoped to work with his mother, a nurse, who moved to the United States in 1990, following a well-worn path for Nigerian professionals seeking better pay and working conditions.

By the time Ibeabuchi graduated in 1989, his medical ambitions had faded and he attempted to enroll as a cadet at Kaduna's Nigerian Defence Academy, only to be rejected. Had he been accepted, maybe the world would never have heard of Ike, but while waiting to reapply the following year, a seismic sporting event happened eight thousand miles away that would change the trajectory of his life forever.

Meet "The President"

When Mike Tyson entered the Tokyo Dome on Sunday, February 11, 1990, to face James "Buster" Douglas to defend his undisputed world heavyweight crown, he was one of the most-feared heavyweights in history. Ten rounds later, Douglas had unraveled the Tyson myth forever and sports fans worldwide sat stunned. One such fan was Ibeabuchi, who watched the fight at the house of his uncle, "Young" Vincent Oleka. "If Tyson can be beat, anybody can be world champion," a rapt Ike concluded as "Iron Mike" fumbled around on the canvas for his mouthpiece.

The Tyson–Douglas fight caused the young Ibeabuchi's imagination to overflow with images of sporting stardom and immortality. A couple of days later, his uncle casually commented: "If I were younger, I would become a boxer." Ike nodded his agreement. "I never knew someone could beat Tyson, and when he lost to Buster Douglas it made me think I could be a champion," Ibeabuchi later explained. "He's a great man. I never thought he could be subdued."

At six feet two, with broad shoulders, surprisingly fast hands, and power in both fists, Ibeabuchi's physical attributes and work ethic helped him progress quickly through the amateur ranks. He won several local tournaments, as well as the amateur Imo-State Super Heavyweight title, and represented Nigeria in several international tournaments, winning an invitational event in Shantou, China, in 1992. He even picked up a pair of victories against Duncan Dokiwari, who would later win a bronze medal in the super-heavyweight division at the 1996 Atlanta Olympics.

To advance his career, Ibeabuchi decided in 1993 to join his mother in Dallas, Texas, where she had settled. Through Jack Webb, a member of his mother's church, Ibeabuchi connected with the late Curtis Cokes, a former world welterweight champion turned trainer at the House of Champions gym in Oak Cliff. "His mother brought him to me," Cokes recalled in a 2010 interview with Tris Dixon for *Boxing News*. "He was a fine student, learned real fast and he wanted you to teach him something new every day."

Cokes's role in Ibeabuchi's meteoric rise cannot be underestimated. Remarkably, he took a powerful but raw novice and molded him into a technically skilled, world-class fighter in just three years. This was helped by Ibeabuchi's willingness to learn and train six or even seven days a week. "Early on he was a bit awkward," Cokes told *The Ring* in 1997. "I had to take him to school, a lot of fighters are resistant to that, but he never was. His mind is like a sponge when it comes to boxing. I've never seen a man work harder in the gym."

Ibeabuchi's behavior would eventually drive the typically calm Cokes to distraction. But the first few years of his residency in the United States appear to have been relatively trouble free, although Cokes did admit later: "We always knew he had some problems . . . but they were never that serious, and they were always kept quiet."

Ibeabuchi often sparred with Kirk Johnson, a top Canadian amateur who also turned pro under Cokes and later challenged for the WBA heavyweight title. Johnson offered some insight into Ibeabuchi's early development: "I knew Ike for probably the first three years of his career," Johnson, now retired, said. "We sparred all the time because I was a Curtis fighter and he was a Curtis fighter. Of all those times we sparred, he won two rounds—ever!—of the hundreds we sparred. I was always outboxing him, but he was a good fighter, an excellent fighter. At the time I was a tiny bit heavier so I was able to hurt him a couple of times when I caught him. I dropped him with a body shot the first time we sparred although he was an amateur at that time and I was like 1-0."

Johnson is adamant Ibeabuchi's success was largely connected to Cokes's teaching. "Curtis changed Ike," he explained. "At first Ike was doing a lot of amateurish stuff. After Curtis worked with Ike for two or three months he was a totally different fighter. I was still getting the upper hand but I had to pull everything out of my socks to win rounds because Curtis made that much of a change. One of the biggest things Curtis taught him was patience. To start with, Ike never had no patience. After two rounds he would be done. But Curtis was able to slow him down. He got him to throw easy punches for a while to save energy until it was time to throw harder punches."

Thanks to Cokes's instruction, Ibeabuchi won the 1994 Dallas Regional Golden Gloves and the Texas State Championship, which served as a springboard to launch his professional career with a reported amateur record of 27-1. By now Ibeabuchi had also picked up the nickname "The President." Given to him by a group of local fans, it was a nod to Dwight D. "Ike" Eisenhower, the 34th president of the United States. In time, it would become more than just a nickname, but a persona that Ibeabuchi would wholly or partly inhabit, particularly at times of stress or anxiety— or perhaps when it helped him to not take responsibility for his actions.

Ibeabuchi was twenty-one when he made his professional debut on October 13, 1994, stopping Ismael Garcia from San Antonio, Texas, nineteen seconds into the second round. Before the fight, in a canny maneuver, Ike played up his resemblance to the still-iconic Mike Tyson, telling the Shreveport *Times*: "When I was fighting internationally, people said I was a Tyson look-alike. Some people in Nigeria and even here in America, the places I've been, say, 'He does his things like Mike Tyson.' That boosts my morale." After the fight, Ibeabuchi was more circumspect, commenting on his quick win: "This is just a step, climbing the ladder."

The bout wasn't televised, and contemporary reports contain little detail, so we have to rely on Garcia's word for it, but the Texan maintains Ibeabuchi almost got disqualified.

"I stunned him in the first round," Garcia said of an early, fortuitous moment in Ibeabuchi's career. "I remember seeing it in his eyes. After the bell, I turned to walk to my corner and he hit me on the back of the head. I had quite a few amateur fights and that was the first time I'd seen stars."

Garcia continued: "The referee wanted to disqualify him for hitting after the end of the round. But my coach said, 'No, no! He'll be alright!' But the next round I was still dazed. He came out, started punching me and the fight was stopped. I would have given him a run for his money if I'd never been hit on the back of the head."

Controversy aside, Ibeabuchi's rise continued with five more victories over the next ten months, three of them by stoppage. There were, however, some concerning incidents. One occurred in August 1995 when Ibeabuchi fought Terry Porter on a card organized by Richard Lord in Austin. Lord, whose father Doug had managed Curtis Cokes for his entire pro career, recalled: "Curtis called me and said: 'Hey, I've got a guy and we'd love him to fight on your card. He's just got started and we're trying to get him moving.' I said: 'Yeah, no problem.'"

Ibeabuchi was given paid hotel accommodation in Austin and a per diem payment for meals once he had weighed in. When the promoter arrived at the hotel on the morning of the fight, however, he was in for a shock. "A load of people from Dallas had showed up to see Ike fight and somehow he had persuaded the guy on night duty to move him into a suite. Then he ordered a large amount of liquor and food to put a party on. He convinced the hotel I was responsible and was gonna pay for it all. The hotel said to me, 'Hey, you've got this bill from last night run up by Ike Ibeabuchi.' He'd run up quite a bill, probably about $1,200. I got them to call him down and I said to Ike, 'Look, I don't pay for any of this stuff. This is bullshit.' Ike replied: 'I am The President. I don't discuss these matters, you must discuss it with my manager.' He wouldn't even talk about it. At the time I was very agitated but he was insistent." In the end, Cokes told Lord to deduct the costs from Ibeabuchi's purse. "You always expect fighters to do dumbass shit," Lord concluded. "As long as the managers or trainers take care of it, I roll with it."

Nevertheless, Ibeabuchi's retreat into the persona of "The President" was concerning. "Whenever he was in trouble, he would always refer to himself in the third person as 'The President,'" Lord said. "He really thought he *was* the president of . . . wherever he was president of! He really played the part of royalty. He was a wild and crazy dude."

Despite Ibeabuchi's strange conduct, Lord had no doubt about his boxing potential. "A devastating puncher, a great fighter, and one tough son of a gun. I was always anticipating he would be world champion. You could see he had what it would take. And he did what Curtis said. Curtis was a master trainer and Ike had a good relationship with him. He performed for Curtis."

Odd behavior notwithstanding, Ibeabuchi was blossoming. A key early indicator came in his seventh pro fight against fellow unbeaten prospect Greg "Kid Chocolate" Pickrom in Fort Worth. Pickrom was no mug—he'd later win an eight-round decision against Jameel McCline (although Everton Davis and John Ruiz would both KO him.) He saw Ibeabuchi's susceptibility to the right hand, and dropped "The President" with one—briefly, to one knee—at the end of the first round, which the referee should have counted as a knockdown but didn't. Considering Ibeabuchi never got an official count in any of his other nineteen pro fights, it was a feat on Pickrom's part. And while Ike didn't yet possess the imposing presence and boulder-like shoulders that he later would, Ibeabuchi's conditioning was striking, as he recovered from his early difficulties and forced an impressive third-round stoppage victory.

The engaging Pickrom—who never fulfilled his potential, largely because he suffered from undiagnosed hypoglycemia throughout his career—has vivid memories of the fight and the "knockdown" in particular. "It was a good fight," the now fifty-two-year-old recalled from his home in Las Vegas, where he has worked for fifteen years as the yard manager of a salvage auto auction company. "I was winning on the scorecards. I ended up getting caught close to the end of the third. I think they stopped the fight prematurely but that's part of the game. In the first round I hit him, he touched down and I think he got the nod on that. After the fight Curtis Cokes called me up and wanted me in Ibeabuchi's camp. Cokes told me: 'That weren't no slip, it was a knockdown,' and he was right. It *was* a knockdown."

Like several of Ibeabuchi's opponents, Pickrom had nothing but pleasant things to say about Ike, and admitted that during the time he spent with him he saw no signs of erratic or abnormal behavior. "When I went up to training camp with him, he seemed like a very normal guy," he said. "Kind of a nice guy. I don't know what happened in his life and situation." After a pause Pickrom added: "You can never tell when a man finds himself in a corner what he'll do."

"These Bitches Must Read *The Ring*"

n April 1996, Ibeabuchi—now 8-0—split from Boxing Management Inc., the Fort Worth–based promoters who guided his early career. As he continued to knock over a collection of tomato cans and stiffs, bigger opportunities called. The Pickrom victory had come on a card promoted by New York–based South African, Cedric Kushner. Through Cokes, Ibeabuchi had been introduced to an established manager, Bob Spagnola, as well as Bill Benton, an experienced matchmaker for Kushner. All three men would play key roles in Ibeabuchi's career, with Benton becoming perhaps the closest person in boxing to Ike, while Spagnola would continue to work with him in some capacity for the rest of his career.

"Curtis was a dear friend," Spagnola recounted. "A beautiful person. He called me and said: 'I've got this kid who's special.' Ike was about 8 or 9-0. Some other guys had backed Ike initially but got a load of his craziness and bowed out gracefully. I think maybe they'd had an argument or something. Curtis was an old-school guy; he didn't sing many praises—so when he told me about Ike and how good he was I believed him. I never had anything more than a handshake with Ike when Curtis brought me on board. I worked like that for Curtis. I did a lot of work with Cedric; I was quite close to him at the time. I gave the kid to him—no signing bonus, no long negotiation, I just wanted to give Ike a chance."

Benton was enamored with Ibeabuchi from the beginning. "He was quite a fighter," said the Houston native, who first saw Ike fight on a card in Fort Worth. "I soon got to know what kind of a guy he really was and I was very impressed with him."

Kushner was the ideal promoter for a rising heavyweight at this time. His high-profile *Heavyweight Explosion* series, which was syndicated across the United States and abroad, was a breeding ground for boxing talent such as Shannon Briggs, Hasim Rahman, Chris Byrd, and Corrie Sanders. Benton was influential in improving the standard of *Heavyweight Explosion* after challenging Kushner to improve the quality of the offering before Ibeabuchi's arrival. "Cedric had gotten a letter from Sky TV, who carried *Heavyweight Explosion* [in the UK], and Cedric had been told if he didn't do something to step up the quality then they were gonna cancel," Benton explained. "I told him: 'Cedric you're putting on some bullshit here. We need better fights.' Once we started concentrating on *Heavyweight Explosion*, it really became something."

With his immense bulk, walrus mustache, and hangdog expression, Kushner stood out. He was also known for his deadpan sense of humor and his flamboyance—he liked pink sofas and had a red limousine with a full-time chauffeur. One of writer Michael Marley's favorite Kushner anecdotes concerns a show that he promoted in Laredo, Texas, hometown of the Canizales brothers, who were managed by Bob Spagnola. "Cedric invited a load of guys to a brothel called Boys' Town," Marley said, chuckling. "There were all these Mexican working girls there. Somebody said to Cedric: 'Hey, Cedric you ever been here before?' With his South African accent he said: 'Actually, this is my first-ever visit to the fabulous and famous Boys' Town.' At that point four or five young ladies came rushing up to him and said: 'Oh, Cedric! How are you? Good to see you!'

Without a pause Cedric turned around and said: 'What can I tell you? These bitches must read *The Ring!*'"

Kushner's route into boxing was colorful and circuitous. Born in South Africa in 1948 to Jewish parents, he wound up in Germany in the early '70s scalping tickets for the Munich Olympics before traveling to the United States on a boat transporting animals to North American zoos. "Cedric was the guy with the shovel, if you know what I mean," according to Marley. In the States, Kushner took any job that came his way, from cleaning swimming pools and shining shoes at the Fontainebleau Hotel in Miami to operating a Ferris wheel on the Jersey Shore. A canny networker, he inveigled his way into the rock 'n' roll business, promoting concerts for Fleetwood Mac, Kiss, Queen, and the Rolling Stones. He moved into boxing management and promotion in the 1980s after he promoted the closed-circuit telecasts of some big fights such as Ali–Holmes. Middleweight "Irish" Teddy Mann was the first fighter he signed.

By 1996, when Ibeabuchi started fighting for him, Kushner was a mid-level player in American boxing, with *Heavyweight Explosion* serving as the jewel in an enterprise that saw him put on more shows per year, it was said, than any other promoter in the world. Kushner oversaw his company out of a storefront office in Sag Harbor, New York.

Ibeabuchi's first fight under Kushner was a step-up when he faced off in November 1996 against trial horse Anthony Wade at Arizona Charlie's, a hotel and casino fifteen minutes away from the Las Vegas Strip. "Wade was a Midwestern punching bag," Spagnola remembered. "Ike got a decision win. It was not an incredible performance but I already knew how good he was." Ibeabuchi would never fight in Vegas again, although the city would play a prominent role in his final fall from grace.

Four quick wins followed against Rodney Blount, Calvin Jones, Marion Wilson, and Marcos Gonzalez. The Jones fight took place in the glamorous Beverly Wilshire Hotel in Los Angeles and Spagnola recalled that Ibeabuchi had a special guest in attendance. "Ike brought his girlfriend along. She was a beautiful Southern girl from his church. She had a teenage boy from a previous relationship who was evidently very much afraid of Ike."

Ibeabuchi was now 16-0 but, despite being aligned with Kushner, no one was taking much notice of him beyond his immediate circle. He was just another prospect, and one with a hard surname to pronounce at that. Even Kushner was skeptical of his potential. Spagnola recalled that when the fighter would call the promoter directly at his office it would enrage him and Kushner would yell, "Get this fucking African off the phone!"

Lou DiBella—then HBO Sports senior vice president—also recalled that Kushner had to be convinced of Ibeabuchi's potency: "The first time I saw Ike fight it was against a complete stooge on a *Heavyweight Explosion* card. Cedric wanted me to watch someone else but Ibeabuchi was the guy who jumped out at me. I sort of discovered Ibeabuchi although he was in Cedric's stable. It was clear to me the most talented guy Cedric had was Ike."

As fate would have it, in early summer 1997, Main Events, the promotional outfit owned by the powerful Duva family, was looking for an undefeated fighter to feed to the squat and powerful Samoan-born heavyweight David Tua for his latest appearance on HBO. Many saw Tua as the "new Tyson" after he strung together twenty-seven successive victories, including twenty-three knockouts, eleven of them in round one.

Tua had knocked out John Ruiz, Barcelona 1992 heavyweight silver medalist David Izonritei, Darroll Wilson, and Oleg Maskaev. Ruiz, notably, had been sparked in just nineteen seconds. Not surprisingly, Main Events was having trouble finding Tua's next opponent. Amid all this, Spagnola bumped into Lou Duva and DiBella in Atlantic City. According to Spagnola, they asked him to consider serving up his fighter Alonzo Highsmith, who had a decent profile because of his previous NFL football career.

Spagnola rejected the suggestion. "I said forget about Highsmith— he's a four-round fighter. He worked at his boxing, but I put him in with turds and stiffs and protected him to the max because he couldn't fight.

Anyway, I told them: 'I've got a guy for you. Ike Ibeabuchi. 16-0.' Duva said: 'No one's ever heard of him!' I said: 'They will if he gets the fight!' Later [Lou's son] Dino Duva told me: 'Don't ever mention that Ibeabuchi guy to my father again!' I said: 'Sorry, I'm just trying to help!' Then a few weeks later Ike got the fight because they literally couldn't find anyone else."

DiBella, having seen Ibeabuchi fight before, was better informed than the Duvas. "I sort of suckered them," he said. "They didn't think that much of Ibeabuchi because they didn't know him that well. They thought it would be a pretty easy fight for Tua. But I'd seen Ibeabuchi and thought he was a beast. I thought I was making a big fight, although I didn't know it was going to be a classic."

Greg Juckett, who joined Cedric Kushner Promotions (CKP) as a publicist on the same day in 1996 that Mitch Winston began as Kushner's personal assistant, agreed with DiBella. "We definitely knew how good Ike was. I don't think the Duvas had any idea how talented he was. But we *did* know. He'd been working with Curtis for a while and we trusted Curtis's opinion. We took the Duvas by surprise with that fight. I don't think they were expecting Ike to put up the resistance he did."

The fight was set for Saturday, June 7, 1997, in the Arco Arena in Sacramento, California. Most media attention focused on local prospect Willie Jorrin who was chasing a world ranking in his bout against Enrique Jupiter on the same card. "Tua versus Ike Ibeabuchi wasn't any kind of attraction out there in Sacramento," Spagnola remembered.

Cokes did his best to talk up his fighter's chance of an upset. "Ike is the most dedicated fighter I've ever had," he told the *Sacramento Bee*. "[He] is a warrior; he comes to fight. He's a complete package—he punches well, boxes well, has great stamina and a great chin. But Ike's biggest asset is his desire to become a world champion."

Ibeabuchi radiated confidence, claiming he was enjoying his dark-horse status. "I have to thank Tua for taking a risk against me," he added. "I think of Muhammad Ali and look at Tua as someone with a Sonny

Liston reputation. We both can punch, but I can also adapt and box." In appearance as well as demeanor, of course, Ibeabuchi resembled Liston far more than Ali.

Kevin Barry, Tua's manager and later his trainer, scoffed at Ike's confidence saying that, "Ibeabuchi will find out that no one will ever hit him as hard as David will." Years later, however, Barry admitted that he found Ibeabuchi unnerving. "He seemed a little strange," the New Zealander recalled. "He had maybe ten guys in African attire who turned up with him. They were singing and very jovial, but Ike was very serious. He didn't come across as a nice or pleasant guy—his attitude was very much, 'this is serious stuff. We're going to war.' He didn't smile and shake your hand. He was totally intense. And that intensity made him a little scary."

Nevertheless, the statistics favored Tua overwhelmingly. Ibeabuchi's three years, sixteen fights, and fifty-six rounds of professional experience were dwarfed by Tua's four years, twenty-seven fights, and ninety-nine rounds. The press, the crowd, and the bookmakers all backed the Samoan.

But Ike Ibeabuchi would channel the spirit of the Pistor Killer and prove everyone wrong.

War in Sacramento

Despite the mental chaos that overwhelmed him so often, Ibeabuchi always possessed one incredible talent—the ability to remain calm in the prize ring. A psychologist may have theorized that it was the only place that gave him peace and freed him from the mental torture and dueling personas that afflicted him. "It's bizarre," Eric Bottjer admitted. "Although he was unhinged and very unpredictable as a person, in the ring he was about as collected as you could be. The only time he seemed to find normalcy in his life was in a profession that is not normal at all."

The night Ibeabuchi beat Tua is a case in point. "Watch the tape of that fight in Sacramento, and look at Ike up there in the Arco Arena," Bob Spagnola said excitedly, even though the event occurred twenty-five years ago. "All the crowd were thinking he was about to get sacrificed. I mean, do you remember what Tua had done to John Ruiz? He was a wrecking machine! A vicious left-hand puncher, a helluva fighter and Ike was stood there . . . smiling! Happy! So happy to be there! I remember looking at him and thinking, *He's in a very spiritual place right now*. I guess he knew something nobody else knew."

It's undeniable that the Ibeabuchi–Tua fight has entered into boxing legend. HBO commentator Larry Merchant referred to it as "one of the best heavyweight fights of modern times." Merchant's colleague Jim Lampley agreed: "The only other heavyweight fight I ever covered that I would put on an equal level for sheer mayhem and activity was Holyfield–Bowe I and that's acknowledged as one of the great heavyweight championship fights of the last thirty or forty years. Ibeabuchi–Tua was right up there with it."

Ibeabuchi–Tua is a fight whose appeal and fame owes nothing to title belts, legitimate or otherwise (in this case the WBC International strap, an unusually meaningless bauble). Nor was it a fight that was witnessed by a huge or excitable crowd—just 3,378 people were in attendance. Instead, it owes its legendary status to its relentless pace and beautiful brutality, which is reflected by a remarkable and well-known statistic—of all the heavyweight fights analyzed since 1985 by CompuBox, Ibeabuchi–Tua featured more punches thrown than any previous bout, a stunning 1,730 in twelve rounds, of which Ibeabuchi threw 975 at an average of 81.25 per round. By way of comparison, the "Thrilla in Manila," the benchmark by which heavyweight wars are typically measured, had 1,591 punches thrown in fourteen rounds. Ibeabuchi and Tua's remarkable statistic stood unchallenged until 2019, when Adam Kownacki and Chris Arreola threw a total of 2,172 punches in a heavyweight brawl at Brooklyn's Barclays Center. "I was at both fights," said CompuBox owner Bob Canobbio, "and the punches thrown and landed by Tua and Ibeabuchi were much more punishing than those landed by Kownacki and Arreola. The exchanges between Ibeabuchi and Tua were just so intense."

Another aspect that made the fight so memorable was that the underdog won, "All anyone [in the Ibeabuchi camp] thought when Ike fought Tua was that they were gonna make some money," Spagnola laughed. "All Cedric wanted was to befriend the Duvas and provide them with opponents for their great fighters. And here we provided an opponent and whipped their ass! There's only a few times in your career—if ever—that you're with a guy who shocks the world. In our wildest dreams we hoped the kid could shock the world and he did. It was a very significant win for Ike and, my God, what a fight! Nobody saw it coming!"

Tua's manager, Kevin Barry, later admitted that Ibeabuchi's performance caught him and the rest of Tua's team by surprise. "I remember looking at Ibeabuchi and he'd really fought no one. His immediate fights before Tua were against Marcos Gonzalez and Marion Wilson. How could that prepare you for someone like Tua? I wouldn't say we thought it was going to be an easy fight, but Tua was 27-0 and already had a lot of good names on his resume. He had really captured everyone's imagination going into that fight and everyone was very excited." In fact, Main Events was so eager to keep Tua's momentum going that they pressed ahead with the fight despite the fact Tua had a rapidly worsening problem with his left elbow. "He had a lot of pain in that left elbow," Barry revealed. "Before his last couple of fights, we'd been shooting him up with cortisone. The day before the Ibeabuchi fight Tua and I went to a doctor and got him injected because he had a lot of bone chips floating around that were causing a lot of pain. After the fight he had over twenty bone chips removed from his elbow and took six months off. I still remember that jar full of bones. That injury didn't help, but then I don't think anyone expected Ibeabuchi to come out in the fashion that he did."

In Spagnola's estimation, "Ike didn't have any respect for Tua and his reputation—before or after the fight," and that was clear from how Ibeabuchi began the bout. After the opening bell, he was unfazed by Tua and started fast, whipping in jabs, body shots, and uppercuts. Tua stood his ground and responded, although his work wasn't as frequent or eye-catching as Ibeabuchi's. A minute into the fight, the Samoan caught the Nigerian on the top of his skull with an overhand right. Unmoved, Ibeabuchi fired back a huge right and two lefts. With forty seconds remaining in the round, Ibeabuchi caught Tua flush with a huge left. As the round ended, Tua responded with a big left and Ibeabuchi threw a massive body shot in return.

As Ibeabuchi sat on his stool, Curtis Cokes was calm. "Take a deep breath, you're doing fine," he said. "Don't stay in there all day."

Into the second round, Ibeabuchi's jab worked like a jackhammer, as he battered Tua's body. Referee Lou Filippo warned Ike for straying low. The pace was relentless, and both men scored to the body and head. Ibeabuchi never ceded the initiative, however, and maintained his incredible punch volume. As Tua walked back to his corner at the end of the round he looked both bemused and alarmed. According to CompuBox, Tua had already thrown 122 punches and landed 40, but Ibeabuchi had thrown 182 and landed 59.

In Tua's corner, Ronnie Shields didn't believe Ibeabuchi could sustain such a superhuman work rate. "This guy can't keep up this pace like this!" he reassured Tua. But Ibeabuchi showed no signs of waning in the third. A swift two-fisted assault in the opening minute forced Tua backward. For the rest of the round Ibeabuchi smothered Tua's attempts to land his feared left hook. In the final minute, the two men strafed each other to the body, but neither flinched nor took a backward step. Ibeabuchi landed a left at the bell—his ninety-fifth punch in three minutes. On the judges' scorecards he won the first three rounds.

When the fight resumed Tua couldn't shift its momentum. Ibeabuchi continued to dominate with his jab. Ibeabuchi's constant punching to the body and head consistently overshadowed Tua's work. Toward the end of the round Ibeabuchi got warned for shoving Tua backward with his forearm and elbow—it was only the second time in the fight that referee Filippo did anything but watch the two men hammer each other. It was a tight round, which Ibeabuchi won, although for the first time he looked a little weary at the bell.

Cokes looked nervous. "You're staying in there too long, sonny," he told Ibeabuchi. "Get outside, Ike, and stick a jab four or five times. Don't let him get too close."

After Cokes's instructions, Ibeabuchi fought at range for the opening minute of round five and threw fast, raking jabs. But a wild Tua left hook then caught Ibeabuchi on the back of the head and the fighters once again went to war. Every time Tua had success, Ibeabuchi seemed to reply with two or three shots. For the final fifty seconds they traded swinging blows. As the round ended, Tua landed a big left hook but Ike took it well. Ibeabuchi's punch output fell to sixty-eight for the round. In the context of the fight it was a low figure; but in reality it was more punches than most heavyweights throw in two rounds. On the scorecards the fifth is the first round that Tua won—Rudy Jordan scored it 10-10, but Henry Elespuru and Dick Young gave it to Tua. "Yeah, the judges gave Tua the fifth round," said Spagnola later. "He didn't earn it but they had to give him something."

Tua's corner was heartened. "That's the way you fight!" Duva said, with Shields adding, "You hurt him a couple of times there, Tua! He's hurt, baby! Tua, let the hook go now!"

Cokes, meanwhile, tried desperately to dissuade Ibeabuchi from going to war. "Fight him inside, then get out of there and go back to your boxing," he pleaded. "You're staying inside too long!"

Tua's rally continued in round six. He threw a big left hook that forced Ibeabuchi backward and then he scored with an overhand right. Ibeabuchi rallied with big body shots and hooks of his own but Tua stalked him mercilessly and won the round.

Cokes beseeched Ibeabuchi: "Don't quit, you know you can go twelve!"

Ibeabuchi boxed behind his jab in the seventh. At times he countered Tua effectively; at others he got dragged back into the trenches or roughed up. With less than a minute to go, Tua landed a big left and right that Ibeabuchi shrugged off. Tua landed more power shots before the end of the round. Ibeabuchi threw seventy-five punches in the round but only landed eighteen, while Tua threw fifty-nine and landed thirty. Tua looked like a rising force.

"You've got to make the run at him and show him you're a bad man," Cokes told Ibeabuchi, a little desperation creeping into his voice. "Come on, let's go!"

The eighth began less frantically. In the first minute Tua threw a hard right to Ibeabuchi's midsection. Ibeabuchi failed to find an opening and Tua gained confidence and landed a right to Ibeabuchi's jaw. In the second half of the round both men started swinging. Ibeabuchi landed a right. Tua landed a left. Neither flinched. Just as it looked like Tua was edging the round, Ibeabuchi showed superhuman energy in the final forty seconds and scored repeatedly with his left, including a massive hook with twenty seconds remaining.

In Tua's corner, Shields sensed the fight was slipping away. "David, baby, look, you're waiting too long with this guy. He's trying to steal the rounds from you in the last thirty seconds. . . . Now, Tua, listen . . . you've got to go back to the body!"

Ibeabuchi began the ninth quicker and threw a one-two that smashed into Tua's face. Tua responded to the body, but Ibeabuchi established dominance with his jab. When Tua slipped inside, Ike smothered his efforts with clever work. Two minutes in, Tua had some success with a big uppercut, but Ibeabuchi returned to his jab, and Tua's punches became wilder and less accurate.

Ronnie Shields: "You've got two hands, baby. You've got to move both hands!"

Curtis Cokes: "You've got to get mean, son. You've got to get mean or it's going to slip away from us."

Ibeabuchi sat quietly, tabulating his own scorecard.

"Two rounds ahead," he whispered.

"Come on, come on!" Cokes added. "Make a serious run at this man!"

In the tenth, Ibeabuchi jabbed with less alacrity, and Tua found success as he charged forward. Two solid lefts from Tua halfway through the round bounced off Ibeabuchi's iron skull. Ike scored consistently with the jab, although Tua's aggression forced him back on several occasions. In the closing seconds Tua landed a rapid combination. Ibeabuchi replied with hard shots of his own.

Ibeabuchi started round eleven fast and whipped in a left hook and kept snapping his jab. Tua ducked inside and swung his overhand right, and connected twice to the back of Ibeabuchi's head. When Tua steamed in, Ibeabuchi had some success with short lefts, but at times he looked tired when he tried to raise his gloves. Tua also showed signs of fatigue, looking like an enraged but exhausted bull. At the bell Ibeabuchi tapped his opponent on the chest in a show of respect.

"Tua, it's the last round, baby!" Shields said.

Duva: "This is going to decide the fight, baby! You want the fight? You want this fight? Then get the hell out there!"

Cokes: "Three minutes of hell!"

Ibeabuchi attacked and scored with a flurry of jabs. He took a hard left from Tua and swung back with a left of his own to Tua's chin before he went to the body. Tua sensed the round was slipping and stalked his man. Ibeabuchi was content to jab and move. The fighters clinched—just the second of the fight—and the referee split them. Tua then started swinging, but Ibeabuchi leaned back and Tua mainly hit air before the men leaned on and worked each other's bodies. In the final ten seconds Tua threw an explosive left that Ike answered with two huge hooks. For the last five seconds both men stood and traded—without science or strategy—in a final display of defiance and machismo.

After the drama, the judges scored a unanimous decision win for Ibeabuchi: 117-111, 115-114, and 116-113. As for the punch stats, Tua landed 282 to Ibeabuchi's 332, out of 755 and 975 punches thrown, respectively. Ibeabuchi earned a reported $47,500; Tua $75,000. Per punch, each man earned $27.50 and $43.35. Short money for such bravery.

On hearing the judges' verdict, Ibeabuchi leaped around celebrating like a kid, while Tua smiled ruefully. As he prepared to be interviewed, Ibeabuchi raised his right hand, his eyes half closed in prayer: "Thank you, thank you, Father."

HBO's Larry Merchant asked him: "What won this fight for you?"

"God. God first," Ibeabuchi replied. "I told you what has been hidden from the wise and the prudent has been revealed to the babes and the sucklings. I did not come to fight flesh and blood here but spiritual wickedness in high and low places."

Later, he adopted a more conventional tone. "My promoter was trying to keep me a secret," he said, smiling. "Well, I don't think there are too many secrets about me now. This was my toughest fight. I did it all tonight. I boxed and I slugged. If Cedric pushes me toward Evander Holyfield, I will take the fight. If he pushes me towards Mike Tyson, I will take it. I'm not scared of anyone. If I fight Evander Holyfield, my brother in Christ, I'm not scared. Tua hit me with some good shots but ring generalship did it and God was on my side."

Tua was magnanimous. "The decision was fair," he admitted. "I got away from the game plan a couple of times and that was my downfall. I knew he was a tough fighter and I knew I was behind on points. I should have stood and punched with him more. His jabs gave me trouble."

Years later, those associated with the Ibeabuchi–Tua fight, as well as members of the media who covered it, have vivid memories of that night in Sacramento.

"It was an incredible fight," Bob Spagnola said. "With a guy like Tua, all your hard work can be erased any minute, but I don't ever remember Ike being in serious trouble. For those of us who work in boxing, nights like that are the greatest. The nights you do something that everyone thought you couldn't. Sure, I didn't do shit; but I was part of it!"

Kevin Barry, despite arguing that the fight "could easily have been a draw," was similarly effusive: "It was one of the most physical wars I've ever been involved in, for sure. It was a brutal, all-action fight between two physically tough, heavy-handed and undefeated gladiators. It was a great, great fight. Simple as that. Even today people come up to me and talk about that fight. They say, 'Jesus Christ, I know you worked with Tua all those years ago. God that Ibeabuchi fight is one of my all-time favorites!'"

Larry Merchant said the bout raised both fighters' reputations. "With its back-and-forth nature it tested the will, skills, and heart of both fighters. It was a fight that elevated both fighters. The Tua side was very much in shock afterward. They didn't know what Ibeabuchi was about until that moment. Nobody knew what he was about until that moment."

For Greg Juckett, who hadn't worked for Kushner for long, it was also a special fight, even though he wasn't in the Arco Arena. "Unfortunately, I didn't get to go. I remember watching it on television with my colleague Mitch Winston and we didn't know who won. We were so happy Ike won but at the same time we would have understood Tua getting a split decision. It was a massive win, one of our biggest while I was at CKP."

Although Juckett and others found it hard to split Ibeabuchi and Tua, Lou DiBella saw an Ibeabuchi win. "It was a sensational fight, a great fight," he recalled. "I thought Ike won. It didn't really hurt Tua but a star was born in Ike. That was his coming-out performance."

Madness on
Interstate 35

"**Y**ou must not care about me!" Ibeabuchi told Bob Spagnola by phone as he sat in Williamson County Jail, charged with aggravated kidnapping and attempted murder. "This is a terrible place! How can you allow me to be in such a terrible place? You must not care about me very much to have me in such a place!"

Ibeabuchi got arrested on August 26, 1997—less than three months after the Tua fight. Bail for the two alleged offenses was $500,000. His career was in ruins, as was his mental state.

Seventeen days earlier, Ibeabuchi drove his car straight into a concrete pillar on the embankment of a bridge on Interstate 35, a massive cross-country highway that runs from Laredo near the US–Mexico border all the way to Duluth, Minnesota, 1,500 miles north. With him in the vehicle was the fifteen-year-old son of his now estranged girlfriend. When the wreckage was cleared and the human damage assessed, Ibeabuchi emerged miraculously unhurt, but his teenage passenger had a broken pelvis, ankle, and jaw, as well as a diagnosis that he might never walk properly again.

"He called me dozens of times from jail," Spagnola recalled. "Those calls are riveted in my mind. The county jail is not a place you ever want to visit. For that monster of a man to be terrified . . . well you can imagine what might happen to lesser people in a situation like that. It ain't no fuckin' fun under any circumstances."

In the days after his sensational victory against Tua, there were few signs of the firestorm of instability that would soon upend Ibeabuchi. Publicly, at least, he appeared to be reveling in the attention of his victory. On the Tuesday after the fight, he made a series of TV appearances, including a prerecorded segment for *Good Morning Texas* as well as interviews with Channel 4, Channel 8, and HBO. In the next couple of days, Channel 5 and Channel 11 also came calling, as did the national and boxing press.

Amid this growing media interest, the ever-cautious Cokes seemed uneasy with his charge's sudden ascent to stardom. "We're not ready for Tyson or Evander just yet," he said to the *Fort Worth Star-Telegram*, contradicting Ibeabuchi's post-fight demands. "We won't fight any of the big boys right now. We're going to keep on fighting guys who are trying to make their way up the ladder, just like us. He needs about six or seven more fights. The big boys can call all they want right now, but we're not going to take it."

For his part, Ibeabuchi radiated the confidence that the first flush of major success so often engenders in an athlete. "Curtis told me before the fight that my life would change afterward, and that I would no longer be a secret," he beamed. "We had a plan and we stuck to it. I just had to bide my time and be ready whenever the opportunity arrived. I proved that I can take a punch and won't back down from anyone. I try to deliver as much punishment as I take. I'm still learning all the time and developing certain skills. But I can see all of the hard work paying off."

In a profile by Robert Mladinich in *The Ring*, Ibeabuchi expanded on his ambitions: "I am on a mission to become heavyweight champion of the world. Let's see someone stand up to 'The President.' It's time for me to step up now. It doesn't matter who I fight. I can box or brawl, do whatever I have to do to win. The spirit of God is with me throughout all my fights."

Such ambition is not in itself unusual in a sport characterized by degrees of absurd hyperbole. Nevertheless, Cokes would later tell Eric Raskin of *The Ring* that Ike's ego became uncontrollable after he beat Tua. "After the Tua fight Ike changed completely," Cokes said. "Maybe he got hit too much in that fight, and that's why he hasn't been the same. . . . Since then Ike's been thinking he can do whatever he wants. His biggest problem is that he just doesn't obey the rules. He wants to break the law."

Lou DiBella agreed with Cokes's assessment, arguing that the sudden fame and attention helped to destabilize an already unstable individual. "Going from having nothing [before the Tua fight] to all of a sudden having some money to spend—I think that may have been part of it. It was known from before his HBO debut that Ike had issues, so it wasn't shocking to me that Ike disappeared at times, that Ike wasn't training properly, that Ike was womanizing, that Ike was seeing evil spirits. Nothing was shocking to me. I knew Ike had issues although I didn't know that he was mentally ill *per se* in the beginning. I didn't know if he was just a guy who was ill disciplined. But he was never a clean-living, wonderful, trusting, stable person. Ike always had issues, but they got progressively worse. He had issues with his girlfriend and his girlfriend's son. He seemed to have issues with women."

DiBella paused then added, with a sigh, "He seemed to just have issues."

In heavyweight boxing there was madness in the air throughout the summer of 1997. On June 28, just three weeks after Ibeabuchi–Tua, Mike

Tyson left a chunk of one of Evander Holyfield's ears on the MGM Grand canvas and got disqualified in a rematch for the WBA title.

As an irrational act, it foreshadowed the darkness that was about to consume Ibeabuchi. Exactly what motivated Ike on August 9, 1997, remains the subject of conjecture. Some believe he suffered a bipolar episode; others say that he succumbed to paranoid schizophrenia. Some even claimed that he went into a rage because of his position in the latest WBC heavyweight rankings.

Bob Spagnola recalled the heat and summer chaos vividly, and claimed Ibeabuchi's actions sprung from the collapse of his relationship with the girlfriend who accompanied him to the Beverly Wilshire Hotel show in January. "Ike fell out with his girlfriend," he said. "She had had enough. So he grabbed her kid and took off in a car. It was a four-cylinder rent-a-car and he turned it into the embankment of a bridge. He must have been going about eighty miles an hour because he left Dallas at like two o'clock and at three he caused this wreck eighty miles away on the highway near Waco. He was in a rage."

When asked if Ibeabuchi's girlfriend had split up with him directly before the incident, Spagnola said, "Not according to Ike; but according to her, yes. This was at the top of his fame but she still had the gumption to stand up to him. So he went for the way to hurt her the most, which was through the child. There was no explanation for Ike not being killed, other than him being the physical monster he was. Plus he was behind the steering column, where you get a bit more protection. I'm convinced Ike tried to kill himself. It wasn't surgical. He wasn't trying to hurt the child and not himself, if you see what I mean."

The authorities assumed initially that it was an accident. After interviewing the teenage boy involved, however, prosecutors became convinced that Ibeabuchi caused the crash on purpose. The evidence seemed damning. The boy alleged that Ibeabuchi had initially told him they were "going on a journey." But after leaving Dallas County he decided he no longer wanted to be in the car. When he tried to get out, he said Ibeabuchi struck him in the face. Ike then continued driving before he smashed the car straight into the concrete pillar.

Armed with the boy's testimony, police arrested Ibeabuchi on August 26. He began to call around his contacts desperately for help. In addition to his anguished calls to Spagnola, he called Kushner's office frequently. Eric Bottjer recalled: "My first encounter with Ike was on my first day on the job working for Cedric that summer in 1997. I was in the office in Southampton, Long Island, and answered the phone in the morning. It was a collect call from a guy named Ike. I said to Cedric: 'Should I take this call?' He said, 'No.' I had no idea that it was Ike Ibeabuchi on the phone. The phone calls continued all week and later Cedric told me: 'That was Ike Ibeabuchi calling directly from prison.' At that point the public and media didn't know he was in jail."

Even though he had only been with Kushner for a short time, Bottjer had doubts whether the company should be working with Ibeabuchi. He related these concerns to Kushner, but they were disregarded. "I said that despite Ike's ability as a boxer Cedric probably didn't want to be on the national news defending why he was promoting a guy who had committed the sort of crime Ike was capable of committing."

Spagnola was also agonizing about the rights and wrongs of posting bail. "You have to question yourself when you start fixing things," he said. "I mean, how would I have felt if that was my kid? So I told everybody: 'Do not spring him! Don't get him out of jail because he could do something else and we'll all be ruined.' It wasn't right to society [for Ike to be released] after what he had done and talked about doing. Also, he wasn't demonstrating that he thought he did anything wrong."

In September, however, with bail requirements dropped from $250,000 per count to $50,000, Ibeabuchi posted bail. Then news of the incident hit the press for the first time, when the *Austin American-Statesman* published a detailed report. At this stage, the prospect of Ibeabuchi resuming his boxing career anytime soon looked bleak. Williamson County prosecutor John Bradley—known for his tough stance on law and order—spoke bullishly about Ike being convicted and serving a long stretch. "I don't think he's going to have much of a career. He's got one count of attempted murder and one count of aggravated kidnapping."

A frustrated Curtis Cokes declined to comment directly on the case, but did say of Ike, "He's happier in the gym than he is outside of it."

Legal wrangling ensued throughout the fall and winter, as Ibeabuchi's lawyers attempted to negotiate an outcome that would help him resume his career. A Williamson County grand jury dropped the attempted murder charge but indicted Ibeabuchi on charges of aggravated assault and aggravated kidnapping in September, with court papers noting his use of an automobile as a "deadly weapon." Soon after, Ibeabuchi was arrested again for violating the terms of his bail and went to jail before being bailed out again in mid-December.

Booked again into county jail on January 28, 1998, the case was finally resolved in the first week of April. Instead of the felonies he was originally charged with, Ibeabuchi pleaded guilty to false imprisonment, and Judge John Carter sentenced him to 120 days in jail. Williamson County District Attorney Ken Anderson admitted the aggravated assault and kidnapping charges weren't supported by strong enough evidence. "The main issue of the case was whether or not he [Ibeabuchi] was trying to injure the young man," Anderson stated. "Our final conclusion was that he was severely depressed and was trying to commit suicide."

Speaking later to ESPN, Bradley, who prosecuted the case and later succeeded Anderson as district attorney, expressed his dissatisfaction. "It was a very frustrating case. I fully expected that his contact with the criminal justice system had not ended with our county. We weren't able to get him examined, but it sure seemed to me—even if he was a heavyweight boxer looking at making millions of dollars—that he should have been committed to a psychiatric [facility] and treated."

Instead of receiving psychiatric treatment, court papers noted that Ibeabuchi appeared to be "competent" and, having earned credit for good behavior, he was even released with something of an endorsement from jail captain Bob Webster: "Everyone was real scared of him at first. But he was a real quiet, nice guy."

On the condition of anonymity one of Ibeabuchi's team told Graham Houston: "If we hadn't been able to show he was off his rocker, he would have been facing very serious charges."

Court papers didn't detail the terms of any settlement with the victim, although later unconfirmed reports claimed that he was paid $500,000, while Spagnola recalled part of the arrangement was that the teenager "would get a percentage of Ike's earnings going forward."

At the time, getting a percentage of the future earnings of a man possibly headed toward heavyweight greatness must have seemed pretty lucrative.

But, although no one knew it at the time, Ibeabuchi's career was already approaching its final spiral.

Soft Return

After his life in Texas had descended into chaos and the courthouse, it was time for Ibeabuchi to start fresh. The promise of a clean slate began in court, with his mother Patricia telling officials that her son would be moving with her to Phoenix, Arizona, and seeking treatment for depression.

From the beginning of Ibeabuchi's stay in Arizona, a return to sanity and normality looked unpromising. "We moved Ike out to Phoenix with his mom," Bob Spagnola recalled. "I was told that where they were living there was aluminum foil—Reynolds Wrap, as some people call it—over the windows to keep out the heat because it's like 120 degrees in the day there. But Ike's mom also said she had that stuff up to keep the evil spirits out. And this was their place of solace where the mum was gonna make sure everything was alright? That's when we realized we were fucked."

There is often a hereditary factor involved in mental illness, of course, and later evidence suggested that Patricia Ibeabuchi was also mentally unwell. This was the impression Michael Marley formed based on frequent conversations with Kushner. "Ibeabuchi believed what his mother believed," Marley said. "Namely, that the federal government was tracking his thoughts and listening to his phone calls and had taken over his and his mother's minds. Kushner would laugh, but what else could he do? He said he would make a decent fight offer to Ibeabuchi and Ike would say he had to consult with his mother. Cedric would get phone calls from the mother in the wee hours of the morning saying that the FBI was tapping her phone, that something had been put in her dental work, that they were monitoring her every thought. The stories seemed funny then, but they don't seem funny now."

Lou DiBella also saw a deterioration in Ibeabuchi's mental state during the final part of his career. "Maybe he got more mistrustful as he started making money, although it wasn't like he started from a place that was warm and fuzzy. He got progressively more difficult, less trusting. He was his own worst enemy, but then again if this relates to mental illness—which it may—well, mental illness is a terrible affliction. I don't know if he was doing anything to help himself, but he clearly had problems."

The team surrounding Ibeabuchi had by this stage undergone subtle but significant changes. Spagnola was still involved, but in a reduced capacity. "Once he got really hot after he beat Tua I didn't really have much to do with anything," he explained. "I got sidelined when Ike got hot. I know enough about fighters to know when they're over you."

A new manager entered the fray—Steve Munisteri, a Houston attorney. A skillful political operator, Munisteri would later become chairman of the Republican Party of Texas and serve in the Trump administration as deputy assistant to the President and deputy director for the Office of Public Liaison.

Munisteri downplayed to a degree his role in Ibeabuchi's career, and was reluctant to get drawn into some of the darker sides of the narrative. "There's a lot of misconceptions, specifically with regards to me and my relationship with Ike," he said. "I was in a different city; I never saw him on a day-to-day basis. I was also only involved in a portion of his career. I handled booking his last three fights. He had had some time off because he had legal problems. He had completed his sentence and been cleared to fight but he had fallen out of the rankings. I specialized in heavyweights. I was from Texas and they were looking to add somebody to the team that could help guide them in picking opponents to get him back in the rankings and a title shot."

The initial plan was for Ibeabuchi to fight barely two months after the conclusion of his court case, on a Kushner card in Connecticut headlined by Corrie Sanders versus Bobby Czyz. But Cokes, speaking to the *Austin American-Statesman* on May 28, 1998, revealed that Ike's comeback had been delayed. "He's on hold," he said. "He has some personal problems to work out. He put on a lot of weight in jail. He weighed 269 when they let him out. We want to come in at 245–250 pounds for the first fight and then get down to 227–230."

In the end, Ibeabuchi's comeback got rescheduled for July on another Kushner card in Marksville, Louisiana. Cokes continued to preach caution. "Ike's not in great shape. It's going to take him a while. He needs to get his feet back on the ground. It takes a long time to get sick and a long time to get well. He's well enough to fight. He's got to earn some money. He's in a tremendous amount of debt. If he jumped in with a David Tua or a Buster Douglas he wouldn't last until the first bell. He's got to be patient. This is a once-in-a-lifetime thing. He's got to take his time and do it right."

Ibeabuchi's team eventually chose Ike's comeback opponent, Tim Ray from Louisville, Kentucky. Ray had graduated to pro boxing from the rough-and-tumble world of toughman contests. In a 14-20-2 career, he'd faced off against, among others, Shannon Briggs, Monte Barrett, and Eric Esch (aka "Butterbean"). Nicknamed "Stingray," Ray had a gutsy willingness to rumble and go down swinging. "I'm no badass or anything like that but I'd fight anyone," said Ray, now fifty-six. "I never cared who I fought. They'd call me up and say, 'Will you fight him?' and I'd say, 'Heck yeah!' If you get the money right I'd fight anybody. I had a big heart."

45

Steve Munisteri's reasoning was clear: "Since Ike's layoff he needed a fight to get him a bit of exposure and back in the awareness of the boxing community. Tim Ray was somebody who could present a little bit of a challenge but not too much for a guy who might have some rust."

The Ibeabuchi–Ray fight was scheduled for Thursday, July 9, and would mark Ike's first ring appearance since the Tua classic more than a year earlier. Chuck McGregor stepped in for Cokes as trainer. Before the fight, Ibeabuchi's behavior caused alarm as he again retreated into his "President" persona. "For a while he insisted that he was just referred to as 'The President,'" said Greg Juckett. Things culminated at the weigh-in when Ibeabuchi disappeared. "Everyone was looking for him and couldn't find him," Eric Bottjer recalled. "Chuck McGregor called his room. Ike ended up hanging up on Chuck. We were very concerned he wasn't gonna fight. At that point, Chuck said, 'I've got an idea.' So he called back and asked to speak to 'The President.' From what Chuck told me later, Ike said: 'Hold on a moment,' as if he was getting someone else on the line and then came back and spoke as 'The President.' Chuck explained that there was a very important meeting and 'The President' must be present—that the meeting couldn't be conducted until 'The President' arrived because he was the most important person in the room. Ike then came down to the weigh-in."

Tim Ray knew nothing of this, although he admitted he was disconcerted when he first saw Ibeabuchi. "They told me: 'That's the guy you're fighting.' It was seventy or eighty degrees and he was wearing a leather cowboy duster and cowboy hat. I thought: 'What's up with this guy?'" Otherwise, though, Ray found Ibeabuchi polite and pleasant. "I heard he'd tried to kill someone or whatever—but there were no signs [of anything strange] when I met him. I thought, *man, really?*"

Ibeabuchi beat Ray handily—the referee stopped the fight in round one—but not before the "Stingray" landed a couple of spirited shots. Ray took away some pleasant memories and the conviction that the man who beat him would have been great. "Ibeabuchi should have been world champion," he insisted. "He hit really hard. He was a really good fighter. He told me I was a real awkward guy to fight. We hung out after the fight and the next morning he brought a newspaper with me and him in a photo and had me sign it for him. I also got one and had him sign it for me. He was a real nice guy."

Next stop was Atlantic City in September. This time Ike's opponent was durable, Jamaica-born Everton Davis, who had taken David Tua a full ten rounds back in 1994. His record stood at 13-10-1. "Ike hadn't shown any ill effects from the layoff [against Ray]," Munisteri said. "So the second step we chose was to get him a larger national audience, against a respected opponent in Davis. Everton was a tough guy that had gone rounds with other people. We got that fight on ESPN, so Ike got wide coverage."

Davis's durability ensured that Ibeabuchi got some needed ring time. The fight lasted until the ninth when Ike dropped Davis with a vicious left to the body. "Ike performed really well," Munisteri said. "[The Davis fight] served the purpose of getting him some rounds and also sending a statement to the heavyweight division that he still had a big skill level."

The idea was to keep Ibeabuchi as active as possible, and to this end a possible rematch with Tua was floated. Ron Borges of the *Boston Globe* reported the rumor that Tua turned down the fight, as well as the counter-rumor that the Duvas claimed it was Ibeabuchi's demand for $500,000 that stymied the fight. Instead, Ibeabuchi looked set to appear on a *Heavyweight Explosion* card on December 8 in New York against Frankie Swindell. As the fight drew closer, however, he withdrew after demanding a larger purse, a request Kushner refused.

Just before Christmas two events occurred that would shape the rest of Ibeabuchi's career. First, Chris Byrd—a hugely talented silver medalist at middleweight in the 1992 Barcelona Olympics, now campaigning at heavyweight—left Main Events and signed with Kushner. Michael Katz of the New York *Daily News* reported that Kushner was aiming to give Byrd a January 1999 tune-up before an Ibeabuchi contest later in the year.

"People were avoiding Byrd," Munisteri recalled. "He had a very difficult style, many people wanted to stay away from him. But that was a fight we could make precisely *because* everybody was staying away from Byrd."

With Kushner prepared to risk Ibeabuchi's reputation and unbeaten record against a slickster like Byrd—in a fight that was as good as even money—some speculated that the promoter's patience with "The President" was waning. Likely aggrieved by this slight, Ibeabuchi brooded dangerously, cultivating his sense of resentment and entitlement.

Just before Christmas he was in Las Vegas, staying at the Treasure Island Hotel. There, in one of the 2,884 rooms that lurked beneath a grotesque skull and crossed swords sign, Ike picked up the phone and ordered a prostitute.

"I have had sex with escorts many times," he would later tell Tim Graham of ESPN. "It's no strings attached. I paid with checks and credit cards. It was a guilty pleasure."

The encounter ended with Ibeabuchi being accused of sexual assault. The Clark County District Attorney's office felt there was a lack of evidence and abandoned the case. But a dangerous pattern of behavior was emerging.

The Baddest Man
in Boxing

From the moment the Byrd–Ibeabuchi fight was announced in January 1999, a smooth promotion looked unlikely. Privately, many in the Ibeabuchi camp knew Ike's mental state was bad. If he made it into the ring at the Emerald Queen Casino, Tacoma, Washington, on the scheduled fight night of March 20 it would be a miracle.

Publicly, Steve Munisteri maintained a brave face, raging against the perception that Ibeabuchi was a loose cannon. "Ike has no criminal charges against him, no serious charges ended up sticking, just a misdemeanor," he told Graham Houston. "He had an incident with the law, it's resolved, and we move on." Privately, however, Munisteri knew Ibeabuchi's preparations were unraveling and becoming more chaotic by the day. They also had a disturbing undercurrent of menace.

"Ike started to act very strangely when we were training for the fight with Byrd," Bob Spagnola said. "Everybody was talking about how unstable he was, although their vernacular was never as gracious as to use the word 'unstable.'"

Greg Juckett added: "Only people within CKP knew, but we were really having trouble controlling Ike's habits at that point. I don't think anybody really knew why he was acting the way he was."

An incident that captured the unsettling atmosphere that had enveloped Ibeabuchi later became one of the most legendary anecdotes about the fighter. According to Lou DiBella, it occurred before Ibeabuchi's fight against Everton Davis in Atlantic City in September 1998, when Kushner received a disturbing phone call. Ibeabuchi's mother, Patricia, who was with her son in his hotel, was on the line.

"She called Cedric saying that evil spirits were coming in through the air conditioning system," DiBella, who was with Kushner, explained. "She said that we had to do something because they couldn't control the air conditioning. Cedric's first reaction was to tell her to turn off the air conditioning. When that didn't suffice Cedric had to call the hotel to get them to turn off the air circulation. There was a lot of weirdness going on. Ike had a dark story line, man."

If his camp hoped a degree of normalcy might return when Ibeabuchi began sparring on February 18 in Phoenix, Arizona, then they were to be disappointed. Ike's first sparring session was with a Pensacola fighter named Ezra Sellers, and it soon turned vicious. Ibeabuchi was cut over his eyelid after Sellers landed a right jab and left uppercut. After the sparring, Ibeabuchi noticed Sellers had a wedding ring on and accused him of using it to deliberately injure him.

As Eric Bottjer pointed out, Ibeabuchi's theory made no rational sense, but then again Ike no longer seemed to be rational. "It was nuts because even if Sellers had been wearing the ring while sparring, which he wasn't, they had gloves on. Anyway, Ike attacked Ezra. In the melee Curtis was injured. From that point on, Ike did not spar any rounds for the Byrd fight. He often didn't even go to the gym at all I was told later. He did roadwork and whatever but that was it. Curtis didn't really have control of Ike by now. Nobody did."

Assistant trainer Jay Wilson also got injured and Sellers sustained a cruciate ligament injury in his right knee that later required an operation. An upset Cokes apparently quit for a while but was persuaded to return. Wilson launched legal action, although he ended up dropping it.

Sellers's account of the incident that appeared in *The Ring* added to Ibeabuchi's growing reputation. "When he came into the gym he was on his cell phone, arguing with his manager," Sellers said. "Ike had a little attitude. I don't know if he was frustrated or what, but he really came at me like he was seriously trying to hurt me. He was throwing wild punches."

Sellers claimed that, a few minutes after sparring, Wilson removed his hand wraps and he then put his wedding ring back on. When Ibeabuchi noticed the ring he yelled: "He has a ring on, he has a ring on!" Sellers claimed Ibeabuchi then seized his left hand and twisted his ring finger "as if he was trying to break it," before kicking him in the right leg. After Sellers fell to the floor, Ibeabuchi straddled him and punched him repeatedly until Cokes and Wilson stepped in.

"I got up and said: 'Your own trainer wrapped my hands. Why do you think he would do something like that to you?'" Sellers continued. "Then Ike went at Jay. He was still yelling and screaming, and acting like a twelve year old. He believes everyone is his enemy. That's his take on life."

With Ibeabuchi's sanity and stability on the edge and the Byrd fight in danger of collapse, HBO got jittery. "HBO required us to bring a substitute in. Ray Anis was paid a good amount of money to stand by," Bottjer explained. "We were nervous if Ike would even turn up."

Kushner, desperate to save the promotion, pleaded with his former matchmaker Bill Benton to keep tabs on Ibeabuchi and make sure that he reached Tacoma. It was a smart move because Ibeabuchi trusted and respected Benton, and the two men had a bond. Although no longer on the CKP payroll, Benton was happy to help, particularly given his affection for Ibeabuchi. "Bill was the one guy Cedric had that Ike was good with," Spagnola said. The friendship between the mercurial boxer and the gruff and tough Benton, an accomplished trainer as well as matchmaker, was an odd but solid one. Even today, Benton remains a fervent defender of Ibeabuchi, and insists many of the myths surrounding him have been exaggerated and embroidered.

"What you'll hear from me is how it really happened," Benton said. "I was at all of Ike's fights. He wouldn't go anywhere without me. He trusted me and that meant a lot. There weren't a lot of people he really trusted. I wouldn't work his corner but I would be there and he would say to me: 'Watch the water bottle for me, will ya?' He wouldn't ask anybody else that. He wanted to make sure nobody would put anything in his water. He was a little scared of that. Usually when he came back to the corner I would open up a new bottle, because I knew it was something he wanted. He knew that I had his back, that I wouldn't sell him out. He also knew that I didn't bullshit. I wouldn't lie to anybody. Him and I just got along."

At the time Benton downplayed the Sellers sparring incident as "just a gym skirmish," a view he holds today. "It got blown out of proportion," he argued. "The other guy was getting dirty. After sparring Ike's temper took over. Listen, it was hot [in Arizona] when some of this stuff happened. You're in a boxing ring, you're throwing punches as hard as you can. If your emotions don't take over there's probably something wrong with you."

Benton's mission was clear—as detailed by Mitch Winston: "[Bill] was instructed to stay glued to Ike's side 24-7, even camp outside Ike's door if necessary, to keep Ike out of further trouble and save the promotion. During March, I spoke to Bill every morning to get the daily Ike updates for Cedric. Bill said that Ike was not training in the gym and was not jogging. He was staying inside all day, doing who knows what, and going out at night—with Bill close by. Bill couldn't force Ike to train, and he wasn't told to try. His job was to keep Ike out of trouble and get him on the plane."

Knowing that Ibeabuchi's preparations were in disarray, and convinced Byrd would win easily by decision or disqualification, Winston bet as much cash as he could gather on Byrd—$14,000 from credit card cash advances plus $8,000 from one of his best friends. He stood to land $55,000 if Byrd won. And if he lost? "We would be broke and crippled with debt."

When Benton heard about Winston's plan he was infuriated. "[Mitch] asked me: 'Bill, who's gonna win this fight?'" Benton recalled. "He respected what I had to say. I said: 'I *know* who is gonna win the fight. Ike is.' He kinda looked at me in a funny way. And I said: 'Mitch, what's the matter?' Turns out he'd gambled a lot of money on Chris. I said to him: 'Well, you're gonna lose it and don't ever ask me anything else about another fighter again, not when you did what you just did.'"

Benton seemed to be the only one who had faith in Ibeabuchi. "At this point all people wanted was to have the fight go ahead," said Bob Spagnola. "Everyone knew Byrd was gonna beat him. Ike hadn't sparred a day from after the Sellers situation right up until the fight itself. And when you don't spar your timing is off—which is so important, particularly against a slickster like Byrd. The feeling was Ike would follow him around for a few rounds, start puffing and that would be it."

In early March, the extent of the chaos in Ibeabuchi's camp—until then a closely guarded secret—exploded in the media. Following up on a scoop from journalist Pedro Fernandez about the Sellers incident, Michael Katz of the New York *Daily News*, wrote a story titled "Ibeabuchi Gives Boxing a Black Eye," which addressed the issue of Ibeabuchi's mental health. In addition to breaking news of the sparring incident to the wider public, the article looked at Ibeabuchi's troubled mind. Perhaps because they were frustrated with their fighter's lack of discipline, Kushner and Munisteri made no effort to hide Ibeabuchi's issues. Kushner told Katz that in his opinion Ibeabuchi was "manic depressive" and recounted the story of the demons in the air conditioning. Munisteri, meanwhile, said that he believed Ibeabuchi was "severely depressed" and speculated that during the car incident the previous year he may have thought he was being chased by "demons," although he also added "to this day Ike doesn't remember what happened." Of the dustup with Sellers, Munisteri speculated that Ibeabuchi reacted as he did because he was worried a "$300,000 payday was about to go out the door." Only the steadfast Benton refused to be drawn into criticizing Ibeabuchi, saying, "There's nothing wrong, mentally or physically."

The article ignited a media furor and by the time the press descended on the port city of Tacoma, Ibeabuchi was now seen as a reincarnation of Sonny Liston—"Mad, Bad, and Dangerous to Know," read the headline for a feature piece on the fight that Graham Houston wrote for *Boxing Monthly*.

Anticipation was high. When "The President" emerged for the prefight press conference, who knew what sort of unhinged beast would appear? There was a problem, though—when Ibeabuchi's flight landed at Seattle-Tacoma International, he wasn't on it.

"You're Fighting a Crazy Man"

When he was slated to arrive in Tacoma for his heavyweight showdown with Chris Byrd, Ike Ibeabuchi sat with Bill Benton over 800 miles southeast, in the departure lounge of Salt Lake City International Airport. "They were flying from Phoenix to Tacoma and had a stop-off in Salt Lake City," Spagnola recalled. "Then Ike decided—and it was just Bill and Ike there—'No, Bill, I'm not getting on any more planes. The spirits have told me I can't get on another plane.'"

With Ibeabuchi so close to a shot at the heavyweight title, Benton refused to give in. "He didn't like to fly to begin with," Benton said. "We were about halfway and had a connecting flight when Ike said, 'My spirit tells me not to get on this plane.' We missed two connecting flights and were just sitting in the airport. Eventually I said: 'Listen, we're gonna do one of two things: get on the plane or go back home.' Ike turned to me and said: 'Bill, if you tell me to get on the plane, I'll get on it, but I'm telling you now, my spirit is telling me not to get on this plane.' I said: 'Well we've missed two other ones. So let's get on this plane and go.' We got on the plane and had a real bumpy flight. I thought, *Oh no, Ike's gonna be up my ass about this.* Sure enough, in Seattle we got off the plane and he looked at me and said: 'My spirit was right.' I said: 'Hey, I don't have a spirit!'"

Mitch Winston—with $22,000 staked on Ibeabuchi to lose—vividly remembers seeing Ike arrive with Benton at the Emerald Hotel and Casino. "[Ike] was shirtless, with a toothpick in his mouth, wearing jeans and a jean jacket, a black cowboy hat, dark sunglasses, and cowboy boots. He was pissed at the world, intense and unsmiling." Winston also noted that, despite his lack of sparring, Ibeabuchi looked in terrific shape. "His dark aura and ripped physique reminded me of Clubber Lang from *Rocky III*. It dawned on me he must have been training alone [like] Clubber Lang, in the private confines of his apartment, away from all conspiracies and demonic forces."

Ron Scott Stevens, who had joined CKP in December as a matchmaker, admitted he avoided Ibeabuchi whenever he could during fight week. "The whole week I was like, 'Please, let me stay away from this guy!' One day they asked me to bring up some lunch for him. I knocked on the door and couldn't wait to get the hell away. He was a hard guy to be around. He was intimidating and frightening. You never knew what he was gonna do or say. I saw Sonny Liston when I was eleven years old, I guess it must have been when he fought [Floyd] Patterson, and when I saw Ibeabuchi I saw Liston. Liston was this mysterious guy who was supposedly controlled by the Mob and was very sinister. Ibeabuchi had that dark aura around him as well."

Throughout fight week, Ibeabuchi's behavior shifted between eccentric and unnerving. Each morning he left his hotel room and marched up and down the hotel parking lot like a soldier preparing for war. Winston witnessed the spectacle with disquiet. "In my view, Ike really thought he was a soldier in the military, going into a 'kill-or-be-killed' battle."

Byrd also noted Ibeabuchi's military-style spectacle. "When we got to the hotel, he [Ibeabuchi] was outside looking at the sky, walking back and forth," Byrd remembered. "My father looked at me and said: 'You're fighting a crazy man. There's something wrong with him. He's just out there walking up and down, looking at the sky.' My whole team, my wife, everybody, we were like, that's very strange."

Later, Byrd's father and trainer Joe bumped into Curtis Cokes in the casino lobby. The two men had known each other for years. When Byrd saw Ibeabuchi wandering around, agitated and staring at the ceiling, he asked: "Curtis, what's he doing?" Cokes apparently replied: "Joe, that dude is gone." Publicly, Cokes maintained an upbeat, facade telling the *Austin American-Statesman*: "Ike's in good shape and his attitude is good. This is the biggest fight of his life. [It] should lead to a world-title fight." Cokes predicted the bout wouldn't impress people based on style: "Chris makes everyone look bad. He hasn't fought a decent, clean, enjoyable bout in his career. It will be ugly—unless you get him out early so that you don't have to see the rest of that junk."

Byrd's awkward southpaw style and his ability to hit without being hit were the major reasons why no other top heavyweight had yet dared to face him. He had a 26-0 record and was—along with Ibeabuchi—habitually avoided. "He not only beats 'em, he embarrasses 'em," said his attorney and agent John Hornewer. Byrd recalled how confident he was. "I was undefeated, I was on my way to the title. I thought I was the man, untouchable. I thought, *You can't whup me! I don't care! Bring me the best heavyweight! Nobody can whup me!* When the fight was made I told [ESPN analyst] Max Kellerman: 'He ain't gonna touch me, he's big and clumsy and slow just like the rest of them!'"

As the fight drew closer, Ibeabuchi caused bemusement at the traditional "fighter meeting" conducted by HBO. "Ike's behavior was very odd," Eric Bottjer said. "Larry Merchant and Jim Lampley were there. I was there. Ike walked in wearing sunglasses and a cowboy hat and sat down. The first question was, 'Ike, we understand you were cut during training, we wanted to know did this affect your preparation in any way?' Ike said nothing and just sat there for, I don't know, ten seconds. It may not sound like a long time but when you're in a room full of people waiting for an answer it's an eternity. Finally in a very lispy, high-pitched voice he said: 'What cut?' That pretty much ended the interview. They normally last thirty minutes or so. I was checking the time and after only about thirteen minutes Jim politely ended it. When Ike left, Jim looked at me and said, 'That man's crazy.' Which he was."

Another meeting served to antagonize Benton, adding to the siege mentality around the fighter. "All the guys from HBO were there and everyone was talking like Byrd had already won the fight," Benton remembered. "I said, 'You know what guys, I don't think I should be here. I represent Ike Ibeabuchi and you guys are talking like he's already lost. I don't know how much you know about boxing but evidently it isn't very much. Ike's gonna knock him out; Byrd's too open to get hit.' They all just chuckled."

Ibeabuchi picked up on Benton's sour mood. "Ike said to me: 'What's wrong? Are you worried?' I said, 'Ike, I worry about every fight.' He looked at me and said: 'I've already fought this fight three times [in my head] and I won all three times. I'm gonna knock the guy out.' I replied: 'I'm glad you've got the security of a positive mind.'"

In his dressing room before the fight on Saturday night, however, Ibeabuchi's mind did not seem positive, settled, or secure. In fact, just as he was expected to enter the ring he informed his team he would be staying put—unless he was brought a Snickers bar. "I didn't see the incident but I was told later that Ike refused to go in the ring until he had a Snickers," Bottjer confirmed. "I understand that Steve Munisteri had to go find a Snickers and then everyone had to wait for Ike to eat it."

Ike then ate the Snickers bar, and the fight was on.

Slaughter in the Tent

he calm that Ibeabuchi had before the Tua fight was gone as he walked to the ring to face Byrd. Instead he projected menace as he moved purposefully through the capacity crowd, breathing out through flared nostrils, his eyes intense and contemptuous. The khaki trim on his black robe signaled that he was in Tacoma to go to war.

After a short bow to the audience on each side of the ring, Ibeabuchi paced around the ring during Michael Buffer's ring introductions. He looked calm as Buffer announced his name, then smiled briefly before he put back on his war face.

A morose Mitch Winston sat ringside, now convinced that his $22,000 bet on Byrd has been a bad mistake. "[I was] next to Bill Benton, who I now wished more than ever had failed in his directive to deliver Ike." When the fighters squared up and received their final instructions from referee Ron Rall, Winston couldn't help but notice the size difference between the two men (Byrd weighed in at 208¾ lbs, Ibeabuchi 244½ lbs) and was convinced he saw "fear in Chris Byrd's eyes."

To avoid Byrd's herky-jerky counters, Ibeabuchi calmly bobbed and weaved and attempted to close the distance throughout the first round.

With just over a minute left, Byrd caught Ibeabuchi with a sharp jab and a left to the body. Irritated, Ike backed up Byrd and launched a series of hooks—but Byrd slipped and ducked away from danger, lingering only briefly on the ropes. In the final seconds of the round, Byrd threw a flurry that was mostly blocked by Ibeabuchi's arms and gloves.

"When you get him on the ropes you've got to find him, OK?" Cokes told Ibeabuchi between rounds. "You're doing alright. Don't get frustrated."

Joe Byrd told his son: "Keep that stiff jab in his face. I don't know if he's feeling you out or if that's the way he fights, but don't get careless."

Ibeabuchi increased the pressure in the second and forced Byrd to stay on the move as he used an aggressive mix of right-hand leads and swinging hooks. Byrd ducked, rolled, and feinted. At one point, after he slipped a punch, Byrd smiled and shook his head. At other times he fired back with rapid, scoring counters. In the final twenty seconds of the round, Ibeabuchi landed a couple of solid rights, as well as a punch just after the bell, which caused Byrd to gesture in protest while Ibeabuchi wheeled away and laughed.

Both corners emphasized finer points of strategy before the start of the third. "When he misses with a hard punch, he's off balance—that's when you get your punches in and then you get out of there," said Joe Byrd.

"When he bends over come under him and over the top with the hook," Curtis Cokes advised.

Ibeabuchi put the advice to use and pinned Byrd on the ropes for an extended period halfway through round three, landing a hard right and several stinging body shots. Byrd eventually escaped back to center ring and tried to reestablish his jab—but Ibeabuchi again closed the distance and, ominously, Byrd spent most of the final minute of the round against the ropes, swinging and swaying and at times countering sharply as Ibeabuchi threw wide, heavy punches with dangerous intentions. In the final ten seconds, several Ibeabuchi swinging shots landed and Byrd briefly looked in danger of being overwhelmed. At the bell Ibeabuchi's face looked ferocious. He looked across the crowd and snarled. Drawing on the energy of the spectators, many of whom stood and roared their approval, Ibeabuchi paced imperiously for a few seconds then sat on his stool.

Byrd's corner worked frantically on a cut above his left eye, but it soon started dripping blood again in the fourth round as Ibeabuchi stalked him inexorably. It was clear by now that Byrd's flurries had no effect on "The President." With contempt, Ibeabuchi slapped Byrd's pawing right jab out of the way with his powerful left arm. Time and again Ibeabuchi forced Byrd to retreat. According to the punch stats at the end of round four, Byrd outlanded Ibeabuchi 71-67 but Ike had delivered every meaningful and hurtful punch.

It ended in the fifth. Once again, Ibeabuchi backed up Byrd to the ropes and, with 51 seconds left, he unleashed a thunderbolt left—something between a hook and an uppercut—that landed on Byrd's skull with a crack that sounded like a rifle shot. Ibeabuchi threw a hard right for extra measure and Byrd collapsed face-first on the canvas, his head bouncing off it. "The canvas woke me up," Byrd said later. "I was asleep before I hit the ground, and when I hit the canvas it woke me up."

Miraculously, Byrd got up within a few seconds. His legs were gone. It was clear from his confused protests that he couldn't remember the punch and didn't know what happened. Referee Rall waved the contest on and Ibeabuchi charged Byrd and landed a punch, but he probably knocked Byrd over with his body weight more than anything. Nevertheless, Byrd's equilibrium was gone and he went down again. Rall issued another count. There were thirteen seconds left in the round, but Ibeabuchi showed no mercy. He threw punch after punch at his unsteady opponent. Some connected, some didn't. But Rall had seen enough and waved off the fight one second before the round ended. Ibeabuchi dashed to the ropes in triumph and raised his right fist. The snarl was back, but so was the smile. As he embraced his mother and Kushner whispered in his ear, the calm returned.

In a tent in Tacoma Ibeabuchi had produced a masterpiece. Byrd's attorney and advisor John Hornewer would later say, "Once he [Ibeabuchi] saw the cut it was like he smelled blood. Then he was coming in like an animal for the kill. This guy is Sonny Liston reincarnated."

Those at ringside in Tacoma on that night in 1999 were awed by Ibeabuchi's performance and still find it remarkable twenty years later. "His annihilation of Byrd was very impressive," Jim Lampley said. "You wondered who else in the heavyweight division could do something like that. We had not seen anyone handle Byrd the way Ike did. I was a fan of Byrd's skill but from the moment the fight began I knew it was just a matter of time. Ike was too powerful and had enough ring smarts and sense to know how to find opportunities against Byrd. The key was to go to the body, and when he pinned him against the ropes the fight was over. It was explosive; it was impressive. It was an electric shock of energy into the heavyweight division."

Larry Merchant pointed to Ibeabuchi's patience as the crucial factor. "What I remember most about the Byrd fight was that Ibeabuchi stayed with him; he didn't become reckless or wild. It was a devastating loss for Byrd."

Steve Munisteri, who was in Ibeabuchi's corner alongside Cokes and Wilson, said that Ibeabuchi "executed the game plan beautifully."

"He listened to his trainer, listened to his corner, went out there and I thought he won every round. The judges were split at the time of the stoppage and Byrd was being competitive, but then Ike laid that uppercut on him and that was all she wrote."

With the benefit of hindsight—and knowing not only how avoided Byrd was before but also after the fight—Ibeabuchi's victory looks even more impressive today. "Remember what kind of a fighter Byrd was before Ike beat him," Greg Juckett said. "No one had done anything like that to Byrd. And it seemed unthinkable [that] anyone would—there was no one craftier or harder to hit. Later Lennox Lewis didn't want to fight Byrd when he was his number-one contender. He steered away from fighting him, perhaps because he was so tough to look good against."

It's a good point, and one reinforced by Lou DiBella. "Byrd was an incredibly skilled fighter. What Ibeabuchi did was an utter destruction of an excellent fighter. And remember, people were worried before the fight that Ike hadn't properly prepared. It wasn't like everyone was saying Ike is in the best shape of his life and he's going to rip Byrd apart. It was a destructive performance."

"Ike was very intelligent in the ring," added Eric Bottjer. "Some people labeled him a brute but he was a very smart fighter, as well as being a very powerful man. The Byrd fight showed how smart he was. Byrd was an excellent fighter who was at his peak when they fought and Ike did not get lucky in that fight—he set him up and knocked him out."

For Ron Scott Stevens the left that Ibeabuchi landed on Byrd still haunts him: "I've very rarely seen a guy get hit as hard as Byrd got hit by that punch. You could hear the punch across the arena. I was right there at ringside and I've almost never heard a punch land like that one."

"I saved his life," Referee Ron Rall said. "One more punch could have killed him."

"I Know I'm Not Crazy"

The jubilant mood in the Ibeabuchi camp soured quickly.

Mitch Winston—who'd lost $22,000 backing Byrd—tried to pay Ike his purse in the dressing room after the fight. Dissatisfied with the myriad deductions, however, Ibeabuchi started shaking his head disapprovingly and pointing his finger threateningly at Kushner's assistant. "He objected to the numbers and asked to speak to Cedric," Winston said. "That was fine with me. I wasn't going to try and convince that man of anything." Winston retreated to his hotel room. Once in the room he looked in the mirror and noticed his white shirt was splattered with Byrd's blood.

Meanwhile, amid the usual backstage chaos at a big fight, Steve Munisteri was losing patience with the boxing media. Graham Houston stood alongside Michael Katz listening to Munisteri declare that Ibeabuchi was "the best heavyweight in the world and we believe he should be the number-one contender with all three organizations."

Katz, however, wanted to tease out more details about Ike's past brushes with the law. "He got a bit snappy," Houston said of Munisteri.

"He told us, 'All we're thinking about is moving forward.' Katz persisted in asking about the incident in 1997. He wanted Munisteri to elaborate on it. Munisteri said Ibeabuchi could remember nothing about the car crash. He then got testy with Katz and said he wanted the media to concentrate on Ibeabuchi the boxer and not keep bringing up the past. Munisteri said some of the questions he'd been asked were ridiculous. He got firm with Katz and said 'No more. That's it. Finished.' and brought the conversation to a halt."

Houston also spoke to Ibeabuchi backstage. "Ike was quite polite, patient, soft spoken. But you could sense a certain danger with him. You got the sense that he could flip a switch if you said the wrong thing."

Ibeabuchi told Houston that Byrd was "an awkward southpaw and I knew it would be a fight. I can see why people don't want to fight him. I give credit to Byrd; he's a man to want to fight a person like me." When asked to estimate how often he had connected cleanly, Ibeabuchi deadpanned: "I'm sorry, I wasn't counting."

Curtis Cokes and Cedric Kushner, who had embraced warmly at the conclusion of the fight, were full of enthusiastic and ambitious talk but must have also been aware that there were no guarantees for the future. For the time being, however, Cokes reveled in the success of his tactical plan: "I knew Ibeabuchi's body punches would eventually bring Byrd's hands down," he told Houston. "He's a tremendous puncher, the best puncher in boxing today. We pushed him the whole six, seven weeks with the training for this fight not to get frustrated. He did not. He stayed under control. He went to Nigeria a couple of times with the right hand but he stayed in America, stayed on the body. Kill the body and the head dies!"

Kushner, aware he had arguably the best heavyweight in the world under contract, allowed himself to dream big. "Ike belongs with the top heavyweights in the world," he told Houston. "The thing that impressed me the most was his patience. He didn't get overly frustrated and that shows a great deal of maturity. I think on any given night he could beat whoever is the best fighter in the world. How can you deny him with that kind of strength? And he can box. I'd just like to get him a little more active."

Keen to build on the momentum of Ibeabuchi's sensational performance, Kushner wanted him back in the ring as fast as possible. Saturday, June 19 was already set aside for a major HBO show at Madison Square Garden scheduled to be headlined by rising heavyweight Michael Grant. Ibeabuchi was immediately added to the card. It was a chance for Grant or Ibeabuchi to get a shot at the winner of the probable winter rematch between Lennox Lewis and Evander Holyfield, who had fought to a controversial draw at the Garden a week before Ibeabuchi beat Byrd.

At six feet seven and weighing 250 pounds, Grant was viewed as the rising force in the heavyweight division. Signed to a multifight deal with HBO, the twenty seven year old was photogenic, bright, and had an all-American aura—he excelled at baseball, basketball, and football in high school in Chicago before he moved on to college. Despite his limited amateur experience, Grant's professional record was promising but his best wins—against second-tier fighters Jorge Luis Gonzalez, David Izonritei, and Obed Sullivan—were dwarfed by Ibeabuchi's victories against Tua and Byrd. Many suspected—rightly, as it turned out—that Grant was overhyped, and that he was a more impressive physical specimen than he was a boxer.

From a business perspective, the fact that Grant was already being lined up as a headliner at the Garden and being paid purses over a million dollars—while Ibeabuchi picked up just $300,000 for his win against Byrd—seemed grossly unfair. However, it was also a reflection of the economic realities of boxing: Grant was American and seemingly wholesome; Ibeabuchi was Nigerian and an awkward customer in and out of the ring.

Despite the difference in their pay, it still was a surprise when Ibeabuchi turned down a career-best $500,000 to face a beatable Jeremy Williams on the undercard of Grant's fight against Lou Savarese (Grant's purse was

$950,000, Savarese's $1.05 million). Williams derided Ibeabuchi. "He's a nut job," he said. "His mind is all over the place."

The decision also infuriated Kushner, who reportedly offered to waive his own cut if Ibeabuchi signed up. Ike was now leaving approximately $700,000 on the table for a fight he could win easily. A perplexed Kushner took the unusual step of enlisting Larry Merchant to try to talk sense to Ibeabuchi. "It was the only time in my career I've done anything like this," Merchant said. "But I volunteered to talk to Ibeabuchi and tell him how important a stage this would be and how it would lead to the biggest things. I told him he would steal the spotlight from the main event. We had a long discussion and, periodically, every two or three minutes, he would say, 'I want five million dollars to fight Lennox Lewis.' Or maybe it was ten million."

Merchant continued: "It was clear that Ibeabuchi had never become fully acculturated into American life or Western life. He didn't trust the system. He thought the wins over Tua and Byrd qualified him for a shot at the title for a lot of money. And in the abstract maybe they did—fighters have gotten championship fights with less qualifications. But in this situation, where Ibeabuchi was perceived as a serious threat who could beat anyone, including Lewis, he had to build his brand, his image, in the public's eye to secure that fight. I kept trying to explain how the American system worked. But it was pretty clear to me that Ibeabuchi didn't quite get it. He just kept repeating that mantra: 'I want five million to fight Lennox Lewis.'"

Publicly, Kushner insisted for as long as he could that Ibeabuchi would take the fight, but held off paying any insurance to cover Main Events' and HBO's costs in case "The President" didn't show. HBO ultimately matched Williams with Maurice Harris instead.

Without the focus of a fight to give his life structure, Ibeabuchi couldn't stay out of trouble. On June 12, at Dallas Fort Worth International Airport, he was arrested on suspicion of disorderly conduct, resisting arrest, and criminal mischief. The incident involved an altercation at the check-in desk. Bob Spagnola claimed Ibeabuchi got irritated because the check-in attendant "mispronounced his name or got it wrong or something." In addition, he was enraged after being told that he couldn't board his scheduled flight because it was overbooked.

"You know what," Ibeabuchi declared, "I am going on the airplane anyway. You will have to stop me." Informed by an officer at the check-in gate that he was under arrest, Ibeabuchi ran. When he was finally halted and told to put his hands behind his back, he refused. When threatened with pepper spray, he taunted the growing collection of uniformed officers by saying: "You better shoot me." They pepper sprayed him in the face. Ibeabuchi staggered backward and pawed at his blinded eyes. The officers pepper sprayed him again, but it still took two of them to wrestle him to the floor and handcuff him. Even when he was bundled into a patrol car, Ike managed to kick the glass window out of the car door.

It's unclear how the incident got resolved legally, but Ibeabuchi was soon free again and on his way to New York for a small media tour, which included an interview with *KO* magazine's Joe Santoliquito, an appearance on ESPN's *Friday Night Fights*, and another appearance sitting ringside at the Grant–Savarese bout at the Garden. As was the norm on such trips, Kushner's publicist Greg Juckett was given the job of keeping Ibeabuchi company. "Cedric would have me kind of babysit Ike," Juckett explained. "I'd check him into his hotel, make sure he had a local contact. He was a very strange guy. I'd go visit him and he would literally be lying on his hotel bed reading boxing magazines and wouldn't say a word to me for like an hour. He was an odd guy and, for the most part, pretty quiet—to the point where he was unsettling at times. I never picked up on him being a violent guy out of the ring or anything. But he was very reserved."

Eric Bottjer believes that at least part of Ibeabuchi's silent menace was a cultivated act. "I think he knew that not talking added an air of menace to him and I think he liked that. It was the sort of aura he wanted to project—I'm dangerous, I'm bad, and you better kowtow to me. He wasn't an engaging guy. He was never someone who asked how you were doing or asked about your family or anything like that. He had no interest."

Ibeabuchi's interview with *KO* proved revealing. In his introduction, Santoliquito confessed to being mystified by Ibeabuchi, writing: "[He] came off as gruff and intimidating when I first met him, but after gaining his trust what I found was a soft-spoken, highly intelligent individual who has his mind keenly set on being the best heavyweight in the world. When he lets down his guard, which is usually up both in and out of the ring, Ike is a very likeable guy with an engaging smile. It's almost enough to make you wonder whether or not some of the negative things involving him really happened."

During the interview, Ibeabuchi's confidence showed. "I see myself as the best," he said. "I can go all the way." But there was also—at times—a dismissive, almost sneering tone to his responses. When asked, "Who do you feel are your biggest threats and why?" Ibeabuchi said "I don't think I have any threats in the ring, because I can go in there and not get hurt." Later, Ibeabuchi displayed something of a thin skin, Santoliquito observing that his voice became "testy" when asked if he feared being labeled "difficult" after turning down the Williams fight. "Why?" Ibeabuchi responded. "I felt like it was my time after the Byrd fight. . . . Everyone knows I deserve a title shot. When is it going to come?"

Santoliquito also asked Ibeabuchi about the 1997 car crash. Ibeabuchi's response was the closest he has ever come to publicly expressing contrition for the incident. "I'm not going to cover up what happened," he claimed. "It's just something in outside life that I was not used to. . . . It was a learning process. I had an accident and I took care of it. There was a certain way things happened, and I learned from it. I rebounded again and I came back. . . . The whole situation was very frustrating. I didn't want to get into a motor vehicle accident, but I was depressed. It happens to every good fighter. I'm no different. It's something that is past, and I have moved on with my life."

When Santoliquito told Ibeabuchi that "some people think you're crazy," the boxer came back with an impassioned, if somewhat rambling, defense of his sanity. "It hurts very much what people think about me. People will call me anything. They will say I'm crazy, they will say I'm nothing, say 'You crummy bastard.' What matters is if you are willing to accept those names they call you. If I was crazy, I'm crazy enough to understand that I need to make a living. If that's how craziness is defined, I like that craziness. I like it a lot. I'm not crazy. I just want people to understand that Ike is in a learning process, and there's no way you could judge him and what he's doing. . . . If people don't give me credit, I have to give myself credit. I know what I've accomplished. I know I'm not crazy. If they say I'm crazy, they're probably envious of what I've accomplished."

Ibeabuchi's behavior in New York before the Grant–Savarese contest continued to be erratic. During a visit to a high-end boutique in the St. Regis hotel with Juckett, he spent nearly half an hour picking out expensive items before asking for them to be boxed up. When Juckett wouldn't pay the bill and a phone call to Kushner asking him to pay also proved fruitless, Ike walked out of the store. When the time came for Ibeabuchi to travel to Bristol, Connecticut, for his appearance on *Friday Night Fights*, he appeared nervous, and even paranoid. "We got out to the street, the car was already there waiting, and Ike turned around to me and said: 'I'm not going,'" Juckett recalled. "I took him aside and I said: 'Why don't you want to go?' "He said, 'I don't trust these people. I don't know who this person is. I don't know why I'm going.' He was very agitated. I managed to calm him down by saying: 'Ike, you're moving to a level where a lot of people will now know who you are. You want to be the heavyweight champion and this is an incredible opportunity to educate the American public about who Ike Ibeabuchi is and what your goals are. You don't want to pass this up.' I managed to calm him down to the point where he got in the car."

As fight week in New York reached its climax, Ibeabuchi brooded ringside at Madison Square Garden. Grant was uninspiring and outpointed the game but limited Savarese, a performance not at all impressive vis-à-vis Ibeabuchi's destruction of Byrd. But Ike's refusal to fight Williams on the undercard deprived fans and the media of the chance to make a direct comparison between boxing's two hottest young heavyweights. Lewis, still looking to finalize a rematch with Holyfield, also sat at ringside and Ibeabuchi tried and failed to get close enough to him to try to hype a potential fight. Security was too tight. And if Lewis was interested in tussling with Ibeabuchi he wasn't broadcasting it.

After the fight, Steve Munisteri and Ibeabuchi faced the media. Munisteri stuck up for his fighter when asked why Ike hadn't taken the Williams bout, a decision that looked even more misguided after Mo Harris outpointed Williams easily. "Why should Ike fight someone he feels is clearly inferior?" Munisteri claimed. "You guys should be giving him credit for that." HBO's Merchant—always a tough questioner—confronted Ibeabuchi with the line: "You're the guy who chose not to fight." Ike responded with an icy glare.

Ibeabuchi had passed up a big payday against an easy opponent, but with Lewis likely to commit to a Holyfield rematch, a fight against Grant was still significant. The victor would—without doubt—be regarded as the most viable contender to face Lewis or Holyfield once the titles were unified. "[Ike] wants to fight the best," Munisteri said. "If Michael Grant is the best, he wants to face him." Although Munisteri initially said "we don't want to negotiate in the press," he eventually conceded that Ibeabuchi would take the Grant fight for $3 million.

Meanwhile, Grant's trainer Don Turner dismissed Ibeabuchi. "Do not mention Ibeabuchi in the same breath as Michael," he insisted. "Ibeabuchi is too small and he can't fight, plus he's nuts. He'd get knocked out by Michael, no question."

By July it looked like Turner's prediction would be tested. There were strong rumors that Grant–Ibeabuchi would take place on November 6 at the Garden. Kushner claimed the fight would decide "the people's mandatory challenger" for the heavyweight championship. Graham Houston in the *Vancouver Sun* said it was "the fight that has everyone in the boxing trade excited."

Behind the scenes, however, it wasn't certain whether Ibeabuchi would even be fighting for Kushner anymore. His contract with CKP was rumored to be up and—as if his life wasn't already chaotic enough—Ike was now in the single-minded and ruthless sights of Don King.

Mirage in Vegas

L as Vegas wasn't always a fight town. Before the gangsters, gamblers, prostitutes, and pimps rolled in, it was an anonymous water stop, a cross on the map where wagons or trains halted for refreshment before heading west to Los Angeles, or east to Albuquerque. The construction of the Hoover Dam in the 1930s changed everything. As legions of bored, young construction workers drifted into town in search of big money and big dreams, the local Nevada legislature—looking to make a quick buck—legalized gambling. The rest is, of course, history.

The only surprise—given the magnetic attraction between prizefighting, gambling, and organized crime—is that it took Las Vegas as long as it did to become a boxing town. It wasn't until 1955, at the old Cashman Field, that a big fight took place, when Archie Moore controversially outpointed Nino Valdes for the "Nevada World Heavyweight Title." *Las Vegas Sun* publisher Hank Greenspan, who helped bring the bout to the city, declared it "the greatest event for the town since the government started using the area for atom-bomb tests."

Ibeabuchi could, in many ways, be characterized as a typical Las Vegas gambler, a dream chaser—like the men in loud shirts and women in low-cut dresses who arrive every year on cheap flights clutching their lucky rabbit's foot or horseshoe charms. How else can we possibly explain his quixotic decision to go to America and chase the world heavyweight championship in his late teens without having barely fought as an amateur? How else can we rationalize his willingness to gamble and face Tua when he was still a sixteen-fight novice?

Ibeabuchi only fought in Las Vegas once, a disappointment for a man with a keen sense of boxing history, a man who saw himself as unbeatable, unhurtable, and a future legend. His Vegas appearance was against Anthony Wade at Arizona Charlie's, a neighborhood casino remembered best as the gravesite of Alexis Arguello's professional career.

Ibeabuchi may not have bet his life savings on black, but he was nevertheless a gambler, a dreamer, and there is somehow a sense of inevitability connected to his career ending in Vegas. It didn't end, of course, as Ibeabuchi dreamed—with his winning the world heavyweight title. The reality—as it typically is—was far more tragicomic and banal: Ibeabuchi's dream ended with his hiding from police officers in a locked hotel bathroom. The officers had to fire pepper spray under the door to smoke him out.

As Ibeabuchi's demons devoured him, his world-title dream—like the dreams of so many gamblers who rode into town before him—proved to be nothing but an illusion. The hotel whose bathroom Ike crouched in as his dreams collapsed around him? The Mirage.

Why Ibeabuchi flew to Las Vegas toward the end of July 1999 no one knows for sure, although there's reason to suspect he was responding to the seductive overtures of promoter Don King. In the weeks since the Byrd fight, there were rumors that King was heavily and persuasively courting Ike, whose contract with Kushner was apparently up for renewal. "Cedric called me up," recalled Bill Benton. "He said to me: 'Listen Bill, I know you've got Ike's ear. I want to re-sign him.' I told him: 'Cedric, his contract is up next month, I don't think he'll be signing with you.'" Benton advised Ibeabuchi to be cautious. "I told him: 'Don't sign a contract with anyone. When you're ready to sign, you let me know. I'll come with you. We'll get you an attorney to read the contract and we'll do it the right way. Don't just go into someone's office and start signing.'"

King, of course, had a knack for getting heavyweights' attention, as Jim Lampley explained: "Any time a heavyweight generated that amount of heat in that period King wasn't going to be too far away. It was a kind of folktale I heard from other people—I have no idea if it's true or not—that King put Ibeabuchi up at The Mirage."

Benton didn't name names, but he did make an intriguing allegation about what happened at The Mirage, saying it was a setup. "Do you know the true story about what happened?" he said. "I don't want to give up any names or anything, but Ike was set up. Real boxing people knew there was nobody around who could whip him. Nobody. They call it 'rule it or ruin it.' If they couldn't be the guys pushing the buttons on Ike then they didn't want him to be champion. I'm not saying who they were, but there were people in power that thought that way. Ike was a personable guy, a good fighter and he was set up, totally. To this day he probably doesn't even know what really happened—but I do. There was nobody else around who could beat him and some people if they can't sign the fighter they cut them off instead."

Richard Lord, who booked Ibeabuchi for two of his early fights in Texas, told a similar story: "The rumor was Ike had stiffed [a promoter] on a fight. He signed to fight and then something else came up and he decided to go with another promotion, a different direction. So the story was that [this promoter] set him up. The next thing he's in jail, convicted and in the crazy house."

Ibeabuchi's mother Patricia would later allege that Kushner set her son up, writing in an open letter published online: "Kushner was hounding Ike to renew his contract with him. Ike informed Cedric [that] he needed to shop around to have a better understanding of what his worth is, and if he matched it, he would re-sign with him. Cedric was not happy with this, because he knew he had been underpaying Ike." Her view was later reinforced by Ike's brother Stan, who insisted that "Kushner went against Ike and set him up."

Other people's accounts ignore the idea Ibeabuchi was ensnared in a conspiracy. "I don't know if you've been to Vegas but it's pretty disgusting in a lot of ways," said Bob Spagnola. "You could be walking with your wife or your fiancée and the next thing someone hands you a picture of a Playboy model offering cheap drinks and an 800 number to call. I guess Ike walked out in front of The Mirage, started making some calls, and the rest is history."

On July 10, 1999, legendary Las Vegas oddsmaker Herb Lambeck—writing in Virgil Thrasher's cult industry journal *Professional Boxing Update*—said that Ibeabuchi was the best heavyweight in the world, ahead of Lennox Lewis, Evander Holyfield, David Tua, Michael Grant, and others. Oddly, and although Ibeabuchi was at this stage ranked number two in the IBF world rankings, the other major sanctioning bodies—the WBC and the WBA—didn't even place him in their respective top tens.

Twelve days later, Steve Munisteri received "in writing" a three-fight deal for Ibeabuchi from HBO. "We'd just reached an agreement," he said. "It looked like Ike was going to fight Grant that fall and, if he got through, he probably would have had a shot against Lewis."

Reports at the time verify Munisteri's account and contradict the idea that Ibeabuchi was about to sign with King, or anyone else. "I agreed to give Ike the number he was looking for and worked out the terms,"

Cedric Kushner told the *Austin American-Statesman* in late July. "I told HBO I would notify them by close of business on Thursday that a deal was in place. Then Royce [Feour, a journalist for the *Las Vegas Review-Journal*] called and told me Ike had been arrested for sexual assault. I was stunned."

In the early morning of Thursday, July 22, 1999, guests at The Mirage called security after hearing a commotion coming from Ibeabuchi's hotel suite. The police, led by Metro Police Lieutenant Tom Monahan, arrived at around 5:30 a.m. and a woman—naked from the waist down—ran toward them. The twenty-one-year-old "entertainer-on-call" claimed that Ibeabuchi had sexually assaulted her. Ibeabuchi barricaded himself in the bathroom, and surrendered only after pepper spray had been shot under the door. Monahan, the Sexual Assault and Abuse Section Commander, investigated the incident and soon reached a blunt conclusion, telling the *Las Vegas Review-Journal*: "This was not a case of a dispute over money, or a matter of services rendered and payment expected. We believe this was forcible rape." Court records later detailed—in clinical but disturbing terms—what Ibeabuchi was accused of: "On July 22, 1999, Ikemefula Charles Ibeabuchi forcibly detained, battered, and digitally penetrated both the vagina and anus of [the victim]."

By the morning of Friday, July 23, news of Ibeabuchi's arrest was broadcast worldwide via the newswires. Even the *New York Times* reported it. Ibeabuchi faced multiple charges relating to sexual assault, first-degree kidnapping, and battery with intent to commit a crime. Monahan also announced that the authorities were reexamining the previous allegation of sexual assault made against Ibeabuchi when he had stayed at Treasure Island.

A despondent Kushner—speaking to the *Austin American-Statesman*—made a half-hearted attempt to limit the damage. "This is America. Ike is entitled to his day in court. Do I want to have dinner with Ike three nights a week? No. Do I think he's one of the best heavyweights in the world? Yes. I'm not in a business where good conduct is guaranteed. It really doesn't matter that my fighter is not the nicest guy or that I might not want him to go out with my youngest sister."

Among Ibeabuchi's inner circle, Curtis Cokes was particularly upset: "It's very frustrating," he said. "Sometimes I can't sleep, thinking about how we were right at the threshold, how he was all set to become champion. And he keeps killing everything we've worked for."

Ibeabuchi was scheduled to be arraigned on Friday, July 30, but, upset by prosecutors' demands for bail to be set at $5 million, he had an emotional outburst in court, and the judge removed him from proceedings. In Benton's estimation, Ibeabuchi's defiant behavior was typical of his antiauthoritarian manner. "Ike was the type of guy who was very headstrong—particularly when people start talking to him like [law enforcement] does or like a judge does."

The arraignment moved, the first of a series of tortuous legal delays that would ultimately drag out the case until 2002. When charges were officially brought a week later, Ibeabuchi's bail was reduced to $2 million. But with no money to pay it, he stayed in the Clark County Detention Center, where, according to Benton, he built a singular reputation: "Another boxer at the jail told me: 'Bill, sooner or later, every bad motherfucker in the world comes here. We get the baddest of the bad. They all land in our jail. And you know what? Ike Ibeabuchi is absolutely the baddest guy we've ever had.'"

The wider boxing world seemed uneasy with the sport's complicity in what had happened to Ibeabuchi. Ron Borges, writing in the *Boston Globe*, slammed his handlers. "Have you seen any of the apologists and 'friends' of Ibeabuchi lately, now that he needs two million in bail money to get himself out of jail in Las Vegas?" Borges asked. "The guys who were pushing him into boxing rings when he needed to be pushed into a psychiatrist's office don't seem as helpful or as concerned about him now."

Ibeabuchi picked up an additional charge of assaulting a jail officer after an incident on August 8. "Even in a controlled setting we can't control him," said Deputy District Attorney Mary Kay Holthus. The judge responded by raising bail from $2 million to $3 million. The assault charge never came to court, but it was a reminder—if any were needed—of Ike's volatility.

Arraignment concluded in September, with Richard Wright, a highly rated defense attorney, confirmed as Ibeabuchi's counsel. He was assisted and advised by Tony Emengo, a New York–based attorney of Nigerian heritage. On September 13, Ibeabuchi pleaded not guilty and a trial date was set for December 6. As the trial approached, Ibeabuchi's lawyers, boosted by financial support from veteran promoter Bob Arum—which ESPN reported to be in the range of $150,000 to $175,000—battled to have his bail reduced and to block the state's attempts to introduce evidence of Ibeabuchi's sexual misconduct and violence toward women from other uncharged cases.

In arguing against a reduction in bail, the state deemed Ibeabuchi to be a flight risk and claimed his "propensity to violence" made him a danger to the community in general, and to women specifically. Nevertheless, Judge Joseph Bonaventure, while noting "a common thread of violence toward women," reduced Ibeabuchi's bail to $750,000. Arum declined to put up the money, but it was raised anyway and Ibeabuchi left prison on November 24 (albeit under house-arrest terms that meant he had to stay in the Las Vegas area and wear an electronic device). Further restrictions banned him from contacting any escort services and forced him to surrender his passport. Soon after, the trial date was moved back to February 22, 2000, after Wright argued that he needed more time to prepare Ibeabuchi's defense. Another hearing was scheduled to see whether evidence of other crimes could be heard in court.

While under house arrest, Ibeabuchi could start training again, as well as field calls from promoters. It was rumored that he might return in a bout on the undercard of the Marco Antonio Barrera versus Erik Morales megafight, which was promoted by Arum's Top Rank and scheduled for February 19 at The Mandalay Bay—three days before Ibeabuchi's trial was scheduled to begin. Two key players in trying to broker a deal between Arum and Ibeabuchi were John "Cha Cha" Ciarcia and the actor Tony Danza. The corpulent and bespectacled Ciarcia—who later played Albie Cianfione in thirteen episodes of *The Sopranos*—was, according to Michael Marley, "a character from the Little Italy section of Manhattan. He owned a food stand down there and a bar out on Coney Island. He once claimed that he promoted forty-three professional boxing shows and never made a profit." Ciarcia had managed Danza, an all-action brawler who had a 9-3 pro career before he switched to acting.

Arum met with Ibeabuchi on December 6, but it was an encounter that concerned the promoter. "I'm having second thoughts," he told the *Las Vegas Sun*. "His attitude is sort of bizarre. The kind of money he says he wants to fight is so far out of line that it's completely unrealistic. On top of that he wants a bonus, and he didn't seem to care what may happen if he doesn't beat the criminal case. I told him all the things I could do for him, but he didn't seem to grasp any of it. The way I look at it now, I'm not going to put good money after bad. I think I'll cut my losses." Nevertheless, matchmaker Bruce Trampler—a longtime employee of Arum's—indicated that Top Rank did ultimately agree to a deal with Ibeabuchi. "Cha Cha did have him and we did sign him," he admitted. "Cha Cha worked with Ike's Nigerian attorney Tony Emengo and we made a deal. [We] got a rental house for [his] mom and dog and him."

As the new year dawned, however, the prospect of Ibeabuchi getting back in the ring any time soon dwindled. On January 31, two female escort service workers from Arizona testified that Ibeabuchi had also sexually assaulted them and held them against their will—charges disturbingly similar to the Nevada case. Ibeabuchi was arrested once again after charges connected to these cases were filed in Maricopa County, Arizona. In another blow to his hope of going free, the Nevada court ruled that testimony from other victims could be heard in support of the state's case. The court released Ibeabuchi back into house arrest and his trial was rescheduled for March. His future looked bleak. "If this thing continues to get more complicated we're going to take a pass on it," Arum said. Within a couple of weeks, Tony Danza and Cha Cha had apparently jettisoned Ibeabuchi, with Danza telling Mike Katz of the New York *Daily News* that he "took a pass" on the boxer.

On March 2, the day before the trial was slated to begin, a dramatic hearing requested by the defense radically altered the case. Richard Wright told Judge Bonaventure that Ibeabuchi wanted to address the court and no longer wanted Wright to represent him. After a series of emergency recesses, Ibeabuchi got his chance to make a statement. It was rambling, incoherent, and unconnected with reality. "The President" argued that he was the victim, that he wanted to be treated like a human being, that he was not a bad person, and that he had always respected the law. The current situation, he said, was "killing him." Could he not pay a fine and leave?

Wright said that in his view Ibeabuchi didn't understand or appreciate the charges he faced and that he had serious doubts about his competency to stand trial, urging the court to suspend proceedings until Ibeabuchi's competency could be determined. Ibeabuchi's mother Patricia also spoke, claiming that after her son had an "accident" (presumably the car crash in Texas in 1997) he had been sent to a mental hospital where she—and he—believed he had been implanted with microchips in his body. She said that Ibeabuchi had undergone an MRI scan in the hospital and "had not been the same since."

Exasperated, prosecutors complained that one day before the trial wasn't the time for the defense to first raise the issue of competency. But the talk of microchip implantation was, in the judge's words, "too much to ignore." The court revoked Ibeabuchi's bail and instructed that he should undergo a psychiatric evaluation before the case reconvened in thirty days.

Flashbacks and Cold Sweats

What exactly was "wrong" with Ike Ibeabuchi?

Bill Benton insists that Ike was not mentally ill, but that he failed to adjust culturally to life in the United States. "He was from another country and the way they did things there was a little bit different [compared] to here," he said. "I once told Cedric: 'Listen, this guy believes that there are certain things out there that maybe move against him. Just like you might believe in God.' Do I think Ike could have done things a little bit better? Yes. I wish he could have been educated better in terms of our culture. Ike's manner was, *Don't fuck me over; because if you do, I'm gonna come after ya.* That's just the way he was."

The concept of cultural difference was also mentioned by Greg Juckett: "I think it was hard for him to assimilate the habits and laws of Western culture at times. There was probably a bit of culture shock for him. I also think he thought—and this may or may not have been a cultural thing— of women as second-class citizens. He was kind of bigoted in that way."

Others argue Ibeabuchi's issues were a result of mental illness. Eric Bottjer said Ibeabuchi was "the only fighter I've ever met who I would say was literally insane," while Bob Spagnola said, "Ike had a lot of problems. He had multiple personalities. He could be a beautiful, wonderful Christian one minute and the next. . . ."

Part of what makes Ike Ibeabuchi's story so tragic is that there seemed to be a consistent unwillingness on his part—and on the part of his family—to accept that he was mentally unwell and in need of psychiatric treatment. This attitude could arguably be traced to cultural factors surrounding the status of psychiatry in his homeland. Dr. Kafayah Ogunsola, a leading psychiatrist who is at the forefront of raising awareness about mental health issues in Nigeria, explained the extent of the stigma still connected to mental illness in the country. "Psychiatry is quite a new field in Nigeria, when compared to other medical specialties," Ogunsola said. "Dr. Thomas Adeoye Lambo is considered the pioneer of Nigerian psychiatry. He studied in the UK and returned to Nigeria in 1954. Before his return, the majority of people with mental health problems were classified as 'lunatics' or as 'crazy' and were subjected to all kinds of inhumane treatment, having been placed in custodial care in asylums where they would often be shackled or beaten."

Ogunsola continued: "For generations, many people in Nigeria believed that mental illnesses were the consequence of angering the Gods, or because someone had cast a spell on you or your family. Or perhaps you had been attacked by a wizard or witch. Those types of narrative existed for years around mental illness and are hard to dispel. And because the narrative surrounding mental health issues is Nigeria is very unhealthy, many people will never accept that a family member is mentally unwell. Some people would rather die than accept a diagnosis of being mentally ill."

Nigeria is far from the only country where stigma is attached to mental illness. Nevertheless, the statistics related to the deficit of mental healthcare in the country are still shocking: a population of 200 million is served—it has been claimed—by less than 150 psychiatrists. The World Health Organization has estimated that fewer than 10 percent of Nigerians with mental health issues are able to access the care they need.

Another issue worth considering is whether Ibeabuchi's exposure—as a boxer—to repeated head trauma may have aggravated or even caused some of his episodes of apparent bipolar disorder. Before the Tua fight, it should be noted, Ibeabuchi had displayed signs of erratic behavior but had not descended to criminality. The American psychiatrist Dr. Daniel Amen has argued that "traumatic brain injury is a major cause of psychiatric illnesses that ruin people's lives," a conclusion based on his work studying brain images and scans. Against Tua—believed by many to be one of the hardest punchers in his heavyweight era—Ibeabuchi absorbed an astonishing number of hard punches. "Tua could punch and he landed 220 power punches," points out Bob Canobbio of CompuBox. "That fight might have been the beginning of the end for Ibeabuchi mentally. It might have started him on the route to all the problems he had."

Rumors have existed for years that at some stage after the Tua fight Ibeabuchi complained of headaches and underwent brain tests. Kevin Barry, for example, recalled: "I heard that after the fight Ibeabuchi went off to a hospital. He had huge pains in his head. He underwent a lot of scans, MRIs, all sorts of things. It was really after that that his craziness really began." Bob Spagnola, however, has no such memory of any hospital visit. "I would have known if he'd had a scan straight after that fight," he said. "But Ike was smiling. I've never heard about that."

Whether or not he was hospitalized at some point, it's worth considering whether neurological damage sustained against Tua might have caused Ibeabuchi to suffer from Chronic Traumatic Encephalopathy (CTE), two of the symptoms of which are aggressive and violent behavior and mood swings. Tris Dixon, author of *Damage: The History of Brain Trauma in Boxing* and one of the few writers to have seriously tackled the issue of CTE in boxing, does not rule out such a possibility: "The fact of the matter is you can only really find out what damage has been done to a boxer's brain in terms of CTE at autopsy. That's when the brain can be cut open and analyzed. They can then find the tau protein, which indicates if CTE is present. But being bashed around the head hundreds or thousands of times, as Ibeabuchi would have been in sparring and in his pro fights, could have massively magnified issues that were already there. It certainly wasn't going to help his condition."

Even if head trauma or CTE did not cause Ibeabuchi's psychiatric problems, the Tua fight may have been a trigger for a bipolar episode in another way. As Dr. Ogunsola pointed out: "Triggers for mental health episodes can be negative or positive major life events—anything that requires you to make a significant level of adjustment both physically or psychologically can be a potential trigger."

In March and April of 2000, the question of Ibeabuchi's mental state was debated by several psychiatrists, as Judge Bonaventure considered whether he was fit to stand trial. A unanimous diagnosis proved elusive, although the testimony of Dr. Thomas Bittker appeared to resonate with the judge. "He doesn't share the same reality as the rest of us in this courtroom," Bittker explained, adding that two hours speaking to Ibeabuchi had convinced him the boxer possessed an "overwhelmingly narcissistic personality that prevents him from perceiving others' points of view." Bittker also argued that Ibeabuchi displayed signs of paranoia and struggled to grasp the connection between behavior and consequences. Later court records referred to Ibeabuchi suffering from "a paranoia disorder with delusions and auditory hallucinations."

Ibeabuchi spoke forcefully in court, but displayed a worrying refusal to accept he was unwell. "I'm not suffering from any psychological or mental ailment," he said, adding in a statement that undermined his denials: "My life is already messed up, and I don't care which way it goes from now on." Despite Ibeabuchi's objections, Bonaventure ruled that he should be sent to Lake's Crossing Center for Mentally Disordered Offenders, a maximum-security psychiatric facility specializing in restoring offenders to legal competency. After Ibeabuchi initially refused to take any medication, a court-approved decision was made to medicate him daily—forcibly if necessary—with 400 milligrams of the psychotropic Seroquel, a medication frequently used to treat schizophrenic patients or those who suffer from sudden episodes of mania or depression brought on by bipolar disorder. The aim was to return Ibeabuchi to a state where he could reach a level of emotional stability that helped him to organize and focus his thoughts.

Months passed. In January 2001 a panel of three doctors decided—by a 2-1 vote—that Ibeabuchi was competent to stand trial, but rather than proceed to trial Bonaventure scheduled another competency hearing to get more expert opinions. Ibeabuchi's lawyer Richard Wright claimed in court that eight professionals had examined his client, with six labeling him unfit for trial. Yet another competency hearing convened in February in Reno, close to Lake's Crossing. Wright complained bitterly about the treatment his client had been receiving, saying that Ike had been confined to his cell up to twenty-three hours a day. A disheveled and despondent Ibeabuchi appeared in court handcuffed and wearing leg shackles, which prompted his mother to complain: "They treat him like an animal. Look at his hair and how dirty he is. He's not being fed. You look at him and me and he looks like he's my grandfather."

During testimony by Dr. Howard Henson, a psychiatrist at Lake's Crossing, Ibeabuchi interrupted by yelling out, "Peace!"; Deputy District Attorney Mary Kay Holthus was convinced he had shouted the word "Beast!" but "The President" corrected her. After a recess later in the day Ibeabuchi refused to leave his holding cell and listen to the testimony of Dr. Bittker, who argued that he should be involuntarily medicated to decrease his "anxiety" and "rage episodes" and to help him "cooperate with counsel." When Ibeabuchi eventually returned to court he declared: "I just want to go home and receive better care. I'm not ready to return to the ring at this time. I prefer people seeing that I have an injury and that would be the first step."

By the end of July, Ibeabuchi's treatment team at Lake's Crossing finally agreed that, because Ike had taken medication (although prosecutors later admitted that "he never had to be restrained and injected"), he was now competent to stand trial. Wright, months after Ibeabuchi wanted him to, withdrew from the case. Public defender Naomi Woolf was appointed in his place.

Judge Bonaventure set a trial date of November 13, 2001. In a further sign that Ibeabuchi refused to accept he was suffering from mental illness, he rejected the chance to plead "Not guilty by reason of insanity." Instead, he ultimately agreed to—and signed on November 8—an Alford plea deal (when a defendant asserts his innocence but pleads guilty in recognition that the evidence presented by prosecutors is likely to lead to a guilty verdict). The deal specified that Ibeabuchi would receive a sentence of ten years for battery, with a minimum parole-eligibility period of two years, and a consecutive sentence of twenty years for sexual assault, with a minimum parole-eligibility period of three years. The kidnapping charge was dropped.

Sentencing was set for December 27, but there was another twist to come. When Ibeabuchi appeared in court he said he wanted to withdraw his guilty plea, arguing that, because he had been medicated at the time of the previous hearing, he had not understood the nature or consequences of agreeing to the Alford deal. The court scheduled a hearing to discuss the matter on January 24, 2002. The state argued that because Ibeabuchi had been medicated on the day of the hearing it would actually have caused "an increase in [his] lucidity." The judge sided with the state and rejected Ibeabuchi's argument.

Two and a half years after the night at The Mirage, the case finally ended. In giving Ibeabuchi a sentence of five to thirty years, Judge Bonaventure concluded: "It's an unfortunate thing, Mr. Ibeabuchi had problems in the past and he had an excellent career ahead of him. Here he is, a ranked heavyweight boxer, I think he fought the leading contenders. This man had an excellent fighting career ahead of him and something happened to him. I don't know what caused this. Perhaps it was his mental condition, but it happened, and it's an unfortunate thing for everybody concerned in this case. I hope Mr. Ibeabuchi goes up and serves the remainder of his time and gets help up there and, hopefully, gets out and will resume his life. But he has to be punished for this."

It was a compassionate statement, but any sympathy for Ibeabuchi was tempered by the victim impact statement that was also read in court, words written by a woman from another uncharged case, ones that described the effect of an encounter with "The President": "I suffer flashbacks, nightmares, wake up in a cold sweat. I had to make big changes in my life. I was fired from my job. I seek employment but to no avail. I relocated. Due to the changes I had to make in my life I don't have the finances to get counseling. This is something I need. The man made a permanent impact on my life. One day, hopefully, I'll be able to get some help and also be able to put the fear this man brought in my life to peace. But until then, sleepless nights, flashbacks, and cold sweats is all I have now. Thank you for giving me the opportunity to speak."

Intruders in the Night

As he sat in jail in the Nevada desert, Ibeabuchi's contact with the legal system had just begun. In February 2003, convictions in Arizona for attempted sexual assault and sexual abuse—connected to offenses committed in 1998—were added to his growing criminal record, although the media failed to pick up on it.

From virtually the first day of his sentence, Ibeabuchi launched himself into a maze of legal appeals and civil actions connected to his convictions—as well as other perceived slights and injustices—creating a constant stream of legal documents going in and out of his cell. Emboldened always by his sense of self-importance and destiny, as well as his indignation at being caged, Ibeabuchi never seemed to lose his belief that he could take on the system and win.

He couldn't.

His legal maneuvers went largely unnoticed by the wider world, and were frequently dismissed by the courts as vexatious, frivolous, or incoherent. Ibeabuchi v. the State of Nevada. Ibeabuchi v. Chesnoff. Ibeabuchi v. IBM. Ibeabuchi v. the World Wide Web. Ibeabuchi v. Wells Fargo Bank.

The list of actions went on and on, as did their dismissal, in a tortuous and self-defeating cycle, like a demented modern-day version of Jarndyce v. Jarndyce.

On occasion, the boxing world would consider what might happen if Ibeabuchi got paroled and resumed boxing. Assorted promoters and managers, often with dubious motives and backgrounds, tried to spring him—and all failed. In 2002, Michael Koncz, a Canadian who would later play a major role in the career of Manny Pacquiao, enlisted a new legal team to assist Ibeabuchi, led by David Chesnoff, a renowned Las Vegas lawyer. "Our goal and effort is to see Ike free so he can fight again," Chesnoff said.

Koncz added: "It's conceivable that Ike could be out of prison in six months to a year, or perhaps sooner." It didn't happen, although Koncz's link with Ibeabuchi would resurface years later.

There was another time, in 2005, when it seemed Ibeabuchi had a chance of being freed. With a parole hearing approaching and influential Las Vegas ad executive and political-campaign guru Sig Rogich advising and assisting him, a release looked promising. However, in a PR disaster, an interview Ibeabuchi conducted with ESPN journalist Tim Graham at Lovelock Correctional Center was published not long before the parole board convened to consider his case.

Ibeabuchi's bizarre and misogynistic statements to Graham did not help his case. At one point he declared, "How can I have the audacity to rape someone I'm paying to have sex with? In Nigeria I wouldn't be in prison for what I did. The system here [in the United States] makes sure someone gets punished whenever a woman cries. This was a call girl, an escort."

Ibeabuchi was refused parole and—in a letter to Graham—made it clear who he blamed: "Tim Graham, you bastard!" he wrote. "You misrepresented my opinion on women in your article, when you promised me that you would be TRUTHFUL. You caused me my parole, you son of a gun! I don't ever want to see you again!"

There would be further refusals of parole in the years to come. Meanwhile, the fragile mental state of Ibeabuchi's mother Patricia was also collapsing. Her comments in court back in 2001 about microchips having been installed in her son's body were just the beginning. In 2007, Patricia—who at this point was still working as a nurse—wrote an open letter requesting help for Ike and posted it on a website she created, www .helpikeibeabuchi.org. She alleged that her son's imprisonment was the result of conspiratorial actions committed by a cabal of unnamed boxing managers and promoters.

"Because of these dealers and their methods, we had to leave Dallas, Texas, and moved to Arizona to seek refuge," she claimed. "Unfortunately, they followed us to this state and the nightmare continued. They tapped our phones, forced themselves inside our Gilbert home, they put chemicals in all of our food and drinks, and they will disengage our house alarm and enter our home at any time of the day of night. . . . These promoters went so far as to . . . bring false charges against Ike in Gilbert and Scottsdale while he lives with me in the same house, by paying a couple of women to accuse him of attempted kidnapping and sexual assault. . . . Since they did not achieve their aim here, they followed him to Las Vegas and repeated the same charges which has kept Ike in jail for six and a half years."

More evidence of Mrs. Ibeabuchi's disconnection with reality emerged in February 2009, when the Arizona State Board of Nursing received a complaint from Dr. Nicholas Alozie, professor of public policy at Arizona State University (ASU). Alozie had, along with Mrs. Ibeabuchi, been involved in a Nigerian Igbo association in Arizona. She had since filed a lawsuit against him and ASU making claims of battery, false imprisonment, and rape. Mrs. Ibeabuchi claimed that ASU and Dr. Alozie had been using her body illegally for embryonic research, having inserted microchips into her brain, as well as foreign objects into her uterus. What's more, she alleged that her son Sunday Ibeabuchi, who had recently passed away, was in fact not dead, but being held in custody by Alozie and an ASU research team, while Ike was also being held in prison as part of the ASU conspiracy.

The nursing board opened an investigation and uncovered a worrying pattern of behavior on Patricia's part. It emerged that she had filed a series of complaints with the Chandler Police Department over several years, none of which had been corroborated by subsequent investigations. For example, in March 2005, she had reported that "unknown occurrences" were taking place in her house. In September 2006, she claimed she found a footprint on the carpet near her bed that was not hers, and that a week earlier an unnamed person had drawn blood from her arm while she slept. In November 2006, she claimed she had been the victim of a series of sexual assaults, dating back to June, by an unnamed and unseen person while she was sleeping. Further allegations of rapes and assaults while she slept followed in December.

Haunted by these paranoid delusions, Mrs. Ibeabuchi had an elaborate system of cameras installed in her house to try to catch the perpetrators. On January 26, 2007, she alleged two men had raped her at her home between 2 a.m. and 3 a.m. after she was drugged into sleep. Police examined video footage at the time of the alleged rape and found no evidence of intruders. Patricia alleged in June 2007 that another unknown assailant had raped her.

In February 2009, Mrs. Ibeabuchi was evaluated at the Banner Good Samaritan Hospital after making various allegations, including illegal experimentation on her by unknown individuals, mention of microchips being placed into her body, as well as being poisoned and being cloned using DNA from her underwear. She refused all offers of antipsychotic medication and did not reply to follow-up questionnaires that were sent to her address.

On June 29 of the same year, nursing-board staff interviewed Mrs. Ibeabuchi and, according to their subsequent report, they said that she "displayed delusional thinking." She claimed that when she woke in the morning she often found needle marks on her arms and that people unknown to her were putting drugs in her stew and then raping her at night. "You may think I'm crazy," she declared. "But someone came into my home and raped me. They are looking for my eggs so that they can get a heavyweight boxer. This has been going on for ten years." Mrs. Ibeabuchi added that people were regularly jumping off her roof and into her apartment and that she was being followed everywhere she went.

Concluding that Mrs. Ibeabuchi was mentally incompetent to continue to practice as a nurse, the Arizona board revoked her nursing license on March 23, 2010. Less than four years later, on February 13, 2014, a few months after Ike's father, the famed Pistor Killer, had passed away, Patricia Ibeabuchi died of a heart attack.

Ike Ibeabuchi's Facebook page, which he or someone close to him seemed to be updating, was quick to point the finger of blame: "The American government should be proud of their wicked murder."

The Land of the Second Chance

I n the decade and a half after he was convicted there were frequent rumors that Ibeabuchi was on the verge of being released. In nine parole hearings over eleven years, however, he failed to convince the authorities that he should be freed, despite having proved himself a dedicated student in prison by earning two degrees from Western Nevada College in 2007, being named on the Dean's List in the spring of 2005, and also studying for a paralegal certificate.

In February 2014, some media outlets wrongly claimed that Ibeabuchi had finally been released. Some reports even said he was set to return to boxing under the management of John Wilkinson and Bill Hodge. As usual with Ibeabuchi, nothing was straightforward or quite what it seemed. It turned out that Wilkinson, who had a 1-12 record boxing between 1989 and 1992, was an acquaintance of Ike's half-brother, Stan. He hoped to manage Ibeabuchi when he got released and even suggested changing his nickname from "The President" to "Train Wreck." Hodge, meanwhile, didn't actually exist, except as an alias created by Wilkinson after he was banned from a boxing internet forum.

In April 2014, Wilkinson confirmed Ibeabuchi was still in custody, being held in the Washoe County Jail in Reno. This jibed with the investigations of boxing writer Michael Woods who discovered that, although Ibeabuchi had been paroled, he had been moved into the custody of U.S. Immigration and Customs Enforcement (ICE) because of his status as a Nigerian national. ICE later revealed that, after a hearing in front of an immigration judge, an order was made to have Ibeabuchi deported to Nigeria. While awaiting deportation, Ibeabuchi was held at ICE's Eloy detention center in Arizona. Nigerian authorities refused to issue travel documents for his return, however, and it seemed like Ike might remain in custody indefinitely in some form of legal limbo. But on November 24, 2015, a post appeared on Ibeabuchi's Facebook page that contained dramatic news:

> "America is the land of the second chance—and when the gates of the prison open, the path ahead should lead to a better life."
> —George W. Bush
> IKE "THE PRESIDENT" IBEABUCHI WAS RELEASED FROM PRISON ON TUESDAY 17TH NOVEMBER 2015, TO GOD BE THE GLORY FOR HIS MERCY AND VICTORY . . . . . . Enjoy your Freedom "POTUS"

Sure enough, ICE's publicly available detainee locator database now listed Ibeabuchi's status as "not in custody." His whereabouts, however, remained unknown. Had he been deported after all? Or had he somehow been released back into American society? The answer came a few weeks later. Ibeabuchi contacted Yahoo Sports over Christmas to confirm that he was out of custody, living in Arizona, and planning a comeback. With Michael Koncz announced as his advisor, he told writer Kevin Iole that he intended to fight on April 9, 2017, on the undercard of Manny Pacquiao's next fight.

Koncz verified the plan and elaborated on the comeback strategy in a conversation with *Boxing Scene*. "Manny insisted that Ike be on the card. He signed with MP [Manny Pacquiao] Promotions with the intention of making a big splash right away. He's not interested in a tune-up; we're looking for a top-fifteen-ranked heavyweight for his first fight back. He was the best young heavyweight of his time and from where we sit, he can still bring that level of excitement to a division that can always use it. Looking at the sport's top level, Floyd Mayweather retired last year and— with his Senate run coming up—this could very well be it for Manny after April 9. The sport needs someone exciting to fill that void at the top. We honestly believe Ike Ibeabuchi can be the one to do it."

According to Lance Pugmire of the *Los Angeles Times*, the man being lined up for Ibeabuchi's comeback bout was Andy Ruiz Jr., then an inconsistent albeit accomplished 25-0 prospect signed to Top Rank (Ruiz later became unified heavyweight champion after a shocking 2019 victory against Anthony Joshua.) Returning to the ring after a long absence against a tough opponent such as Ruiz Jr. seemed like lunacy. But then again, as some within the boxing world pointed out, Ibeabuchi was only forty-three, and George Foreman had been forty-five when he won the heavyweight title for the second time. Foreman himself even weighed in on Ibeabuchi's comeback, telling boxing writer Bernard Fernandez the following: "Physically, there's no reason he can't [come back]. If he really is coming back against a credible opponent, it must mean somebody believes in him, and he believes in himself too. And if he can pull it off, he's right back on top. This could be an exciting thing."

Chris Byrd, now retired after a 41-5-1 career that saw him win WBO and IBF world titles, was more circumspect: "It'll be tough for Ike," he stressed. "He beat Tua in a very close fight; he beat me and that put him to superstar status. Everybody was going crazy for him, but now it's been seventeen years and he's forty-three years old. In terms of his physical stature, he was considered 'big' seventeen years ago. But there [are] a lot bigger guys than him now out there who are ready to rumble. Age catches up with everybody, I don't care who you are. So it's going to be tough, especially in an era of big heavyweights. God bless him on his journey and more power to him for coming back. Hopefully he can make some waves, but it's going to be a tough, uphill battle."

There was some confusion on January 22 when promoter Bob Arum told writer Mike Coppinger that Ibeabuchi was likely to be deported and wouldn't be on the Pacquiao–Bradley card after all. Koncz responded forcefully: "Bob does not know or have all the facts so it is beyond me why he would make such statement," he told NY Fights. "Arum is not the only promoter in boxing that we can work with."

Regardless of whether he fought on Pacquiao's undercard or not, it seemed a matter of time before Ibeabuchi scheduled a comeback bout. As he trained hard, "The President's" confidence and ambition were growing, and the boxing world was intrigued.

An Audience with "The President"

Soft-spoken and measured, Ibeabuchi didn't sound like a man suffering from mental illness, let alone one who had just spent the best part of two decades in a maximum-security prison. The crazed and depraved monster of boxing myth was simply not there. Even when Ibeabuchi was displeased because I had referred to him by his Christian name, he took pains to admonish me gently.

"Mr. Williams," he told me, "Would you please refer to me as Mr. Ibeabuchi? I prefer to be addressed by my surname. I would appreciate that." It was the afternoon of February 17, 2016, and there was a palpable sense of optimism in his carefully chosen words. Although he didn't yet have a definite date for his comeback, "The President" seemed confident that it was just a matter of time until he returned to the ring.

"To be honest I have not signed any contracts," he said of the proposed Ruiz match-up. "But yes, I was hoping there would be a fight for me in April, and I very much wanted to fight on the Manny Pacquiao card. I'm ready to relaunch my career and I'm in good shape. I am eager to return, by God's grace. I'm just waiting for Mr. Koncz to return from the

Philippines [where he had been in camp with Pacquiao], so we can round things off. It's almost time. I'm feeling very elated about the comeback. I want to prove that nothing has been taken away from me in terms of my boxing skills and techniques. I want to prove I can still become a world champion."

When asked to clarify his legal status, Ibeabuchi stressed that "I am not going to be deported. After the Supreme Court of Nevada issued my release, my status as a legal resident of the United States had expired, because my green card expired in 2006. Therefore I needed some assistance with the renewal of my green card. I'm legally acceptable and allowed to stay in the United States of America as we speak."

Ibeabuchi also emphasized that he had been preparing hard since leaving custody. "So far I've been training mainly for stamina and strength. I have reserved the last phase of my training regimen for sparring and boxing training. I intend to prove that I'm in good shape to maintain another run at the heavyweight title. I was ready to fight for the title after beating David Tua [in 1997], but I had to wait. After a lengthy incarceration, the doubts should be erased soon about Ibeabuchi's fighting ability!"

In terms of his tactical approach, Ibeabuchi claimed that his boxing style would undergo only minor changes despite his advance in years. "If it isn't broke, don't change it. However, I intend to jab a little bit more. I want to use my jab to set up my hooks, as well as to protect myself effectively. You can be sure that you will see a very sound defensive fighter when I return. I intend to protect myself as I want to be here for quite a while after I have become the world champion."

When asked to talk about the two greatest nights of his career—against Tua and Byrd—Ibeabuchi's memory was sharp.

"Going into the Tua fight I was confident," he remembered. "Curtis Cokes and I knew we could beat him. We trained to go the distance and we also prepared to throw many punches. Energy and work level were needed to defeat him. He was a formidable opponent, but we took his left hook away from him. I wasn't surprised how intense the fight was, but we were confident in our plan and execution, and the result was unanimous."

Ibeabuchi's pride in the CompuBox record the fight set was clear. "We didn't intend to set any records," he said. "I knew Ali and Frazier had set a record but no way did we intend to beat it. I'm proud of that, though, and I enjoyed the fight—I just wish I had sat more on my punches, especially when I was commanding the fight. Although Mr. Tua was a durable fighter, there's no doubt in my mind, if I had reduced the number of punches thrown and had sat on them maybe I would have been able to knock him out. I would have preferred to stop him than go twelve rounds!"

Turning his attention to the Byrd fight, Ibeabuchi was candid about why he took the contest. "No one wanted to fight Mr. Byrd or I, so we fought each other in the hope of getting a title shot. It was a tough fight in which I risked my unbeaten record and a potential title shot but I was literally broke. I had moved from Dallas, Texas, to Chandler, Arizona. I had no money—there were a lot of issues that I was going through. I had challenged everyone for a title fight and no one had responded. Mr. Byrd was a very good boxer, but the only reason I really took the fight was for the money. I asked for half a million dollars and got $300,000."

Ibeabuchi broke down the tactics Cokes had urged him to adopt. "Byrd had a very different style—he was the reverse of Tua. Curtis Cokes my trainer, who is a legend, developed a plan that I wasn't sure would work. We developed the left uppercut. I'm a right-hander and use the right uppercut, but Curtis wanted me to have the option of a powerful left uppercut as well as a right uppercut. In the first four rounds I moved away from his left as he was a southpaw. Then when I trapped him on the ropes in the fifth, I could unleash on him. He was like a Superman being able to stand up again after that punch, but I knew he couldn't stay up much longer so I went after him."

Returning to the present, Ibeabuchi was adamant that he had no doubts about making a comeback in his mid-forties. "I have unfinished business in boxing," he emphasized, his voice never wavering. "It's more a case of why shouldn't I come back, rather than why I should! My strength is that I have not been defeated. So let's fight and let's see if any heavyweights can prove or disprove my ability. I want all the heavyweight fighters out there to attempt to defeat me or hand a loss to me. I don't see anyone in the division at this time and I didn't see anyone in the division in 1999 [who could beat me]. Most people might think I should have retired by now, but I haven't been a world champion. To me that is an insult, so I have to redeem myself. I want to be a world champion before day turns to dusk."

When asked how he would have fared against the long-retired fighters like Lennox Lewis, Evander Holyfield, and Mike Tyson, Ibeabuchi was philosophical. "I wanted a title shot against the winner of Lennox Lewis and Holyfield," he explained. "Everyone thought that Lewis defeated Holyfield in their first fight and after their second fight I believe Lewis would have fought [Michael] Grant and I would have fought Holyfield. But while waiting for the Lewis–Holyfield rematch I was locked up so, unfortunately, I didn't continue with my twenty-first fight until now. The Holyfield fight did not happen, nor Lewis or Tyson, so commenting on them now would be crying over spilled milk."

Did Ibeabuchi draw inspiration from George Foreman's achievement in winning the world heavyweight title for a second time at the age of forty-five in 1994? "I don't compare myself to Mr. Foreman. I am a technical, tactical fighter and I remain undefeated. Mr. Foreman was returning from a defeat against Muhammad Ali [as well as against Jimmy Young]. Although he was an Olympic gold medalist, I maintain that at this stage of my life I have more skills and more mobility than Mr. Foreman when he returned. Yes, he became a world champion at the age of forty-five but I have a copy of the fight and if Mr. [Michael] Moorer had been listening to his trainer then Mr. Foreman would not have become world champion again!"

Although some might have dismissed such a response as being arrogant, Ibeabuchi's soft-spoken manner and formal demeanor negated that.

Indeed, throughout the entire conversation Ibeabuchi gave an endearingly mild-mannered and friendly impression, which is of course at odds with the image of a crazed and unhinged monster that the media has so often created.

Our conversation ended poignantly. I asked Ibeabuchi how it felt to be free again after being in custody so long.

"I don't know if I am free yet," he admitted after a pause, his voice almost wistful. "I won't feel free until I step into the ring to carry on where I stopped after my twentieth fight. So I won't know the answer to that question until I return to the boxing ring. I can't consider myself free until then."

Fifty days later, Ibeabuchi was back in prison.

Operation Justice

"Operation Justice" isn't one of those quaint Arizonan traditions—like building a tumbleweed snowman or putting a Santa hat on a cactus—but it creates good publicity for law enforcement agencies in the state.

Started by the United States Marshals Service (USMS) in 2008, the annual operation sees the USMS, alongside other local, federal, and state agencies, target "fugitives and criminals" with outstanding arrest warrants and apprehend as many as possible in a period that coincides with National Crime Victims' Rights Week in April. When the number of arrests has been tallied, a press release is sent out that contains mugshots and descriptions of some of the more eye-catching arrestees. Most of the coverage doesn't address the question of how effective Operation Justice really is. In truth it isn't. For example, in 2014 it was reported there were 30,000 outstanding fugitive warrants in Arizona, and Operation Justice saw just 273 arrests. But that's not really the point. Law enforcement gets publicity out of Operation Justice and everyone goes home happy—apart from the fugitives, of course.

As part of "Operation Justice 2016,'" Ike Ibeabuchi represented a media-friendly capture. Arrested on April 7 in Gilbert, "The President" was one of 203 people, but his high profile ensured that his menacing face was displayed in the press release and shown on the local evening news.

Ibeabuchi's return to custody naturally caused anxiety for his family. "What offense did he commit?" said his half-brother, Stan. "I understand that Ike should be on probation after his release but I really want to know how he violated his probation conditions. Ike is busy with his training and has no time to violate the law or conditions of his probation. They simply want his exit from [the] US and some of his enemies can pay any amount to ensure that he is removed. It started with perpetual parole denial for no good reason after he engaged himself on self-improvement programs while incarcerated."

Stan added: "When we [Ike and I] talked, he assured me that he will never have himself messed up again in that manner it happened and what's important to him right now is to rebuild his career. My family has [gone] through hard times believing that some day things will be well with him again."

Why was Ibeabuchi arrested again? Papers filed in the Arizona Court of Appeals explain what happened. After reporting to the Maricopa Adult Probation Department after his release from ICE custody, Ibeabuchi had verbally agreed that he would comply with his probation conditions but refused to sign a form confirming this. Although he maintained all of his scheduled probation appointments and registered as a sex offender with the sheriff's department as required, in January 2016 Ibeabuchi's probation officer requested a meeting with him to "address [his] refusal to sign probation documents." Encouraged by a private defense counsel to sign the documents, Ibeabuchi finally did so; but he subsequently failed to schedule an appointment with psychological and consulting services for his sex offender treatment. On April 5, the state petitioned to revoke his probation for failing "to attend, actively participate, and remain in sex offender treatment." Two days later he got arrested.

Ibeabuchi denied the violation, but the court affirmed the decision in June. The Superior Court was then forced to grant continuances of several hearings after a belligerent Ibeabuchi refused to be transported to court. After he also refused to meet with his court-appointed attorney, the Superior Court ordered Ibeabuchi to undergo a mental health examination to determine if he was competent. Of the three experts who evaluated Ibeabuchi, two found him competent but the third did not, noting he was "illogical, irrational," "lacked insight into his condition," and "was not reality-based in his thinking." Nevertheless, the 2-1 vote was enough for the case to proceed.

Because he refused to attend eight hearings, an order was made for Ibeabuchi to be transported to court "by all means necessary." But although he arrived at the courthouse, he refused to enter the courtroom. Ibeabuchi eventually filed a motion to represent himself, claiming he "had a run-in with [his] attorneys" and that he believed he could "help [himself] better." He also claimed that the court had no jurisdiction over him. The court rejected Ibeabuchi's argument, concluding that his reasoning was "largely incoherent." His probation was then revoked and a three-and-a-half-year sentence imposed, albeit with 505 days of time served applied.

After returning to prison, Ibeabuchi initiated a range of legal actions and appeals, all of which failed. While in Eyman State Prison he worked as a laundry, kitchen, and facilities worker and through July 2020 he had committed eight disciplinary infractions, five classified as minor (including disobeying verbal or written orders) and three classified as major (including disorderly conduct, and threatening or intimidating behavior). According to the Arizona prisoner database, Ibeabuchi was released from prison on September 23, 2020. With an outstanding 2018 detainer issued by ICE still against his name, however, he was then transferred to immigration custody at Eloy, Arizona.

The Dream That Will Never Die

Ike Ibeabuchi hasn't boxed professionally in more than twenty-two years.

But boxing being boxing, we haven't necessarily seen the last of him in the ring. "There are places that would probably let him fight," Lou DiBella said. "If he wants to go down that route he's entitled to and if he was free for long enough, he'd unquestionably get someone to work with him. It wouldn't be something I'd want to be involved in."

Claude Abrams, former editor of *Boxing News*, agreed that an Ibeabuchi comeback remains possible: "What else is he going to do? It's what he knows best. He has a name. He's going to need money. It's quite possible he could make a comeback. In the lawless world of boxing, there's always going to be a rogue state that will give him a license."

The truth, though, is that even if Ibeabuchi made a comeback it would be meaningless. The Ibeabuchi who battled Tua and demolished Byrd is gone. "There are fans who would watch an Ibeabuchi comeback out of curiosity," said Tris Dixon. "They might be thinking that somehow he would mount some sort of George Foreman–style comeback. There would be that curiosity about whether he could deliver on his potential. But he can't—his time has been and gone."

Assuming an Ibeabuchi comeback would indeed end in defeat or embarrassment, let's look at what Ike could—or should—have achieved. "He was a natural," said Jim Lampley. "He had the speed, he had the power, and he had an energy level and an ability to fight for the full three minutes of every round. Everything was there. You don't see that often. To come from Nigeria and achieve that level of skill and mastery at that stage of his development was extraordinary. He was a natural and you don't see pure naturals very often in boxing. Many athletes underestimate the level of craft and skill, the constant application and years of learning that it takes to become a skilled boxer. And he had it. It's a loss to the sport that he couldn't keep his life together."

Larry Merchant agreed with his former HBO colleague. "In the big picture of boxing it's another tragedy. I think Ibeabuchi had the talent and—interestingly—the discipline *inside* the ring, as well as all the other qualities you want to see in a champion. He was an exciting crowd-friendly fighter. He certainly had the ability to be an elite heavyweight champion if he'd had a little bit more stability and vision. Maybe Lennox Lewis would have beaten him, but I want to see that fight."

"He was no more than a year or two fights away from a world-title fight," said Lou DiBella. "And you know what? He might have won. He certainly would have been a problem for anybody."

Bob Spagnola also insisted that Ibeabuchi had the tools to rule the boxing world. "He was so fundamentally sound. Balance means everything in boxing and he had great balance. If you have that a lot of great things can follow. I think [Lennox] Lewis was a great champion but Ike was cut from a different cloth. I think anybody could have been overpowered by Ike. He really did bring it."

Bill Benton believed that Ibeabuchi would have been the best heavyweight of his era. "Ike was the best out there. Period. Probably the best heavyweight I've ever seen and I've been around a while. Holyfield trained in my gym in Houston, Texas, for six or seven years and Evander could have never stayed with Ike. Ike was too good and he was too big. He believed in himself and he trained harder than any fighter I've ever known at that weight."

Chris Byrd was more skeptical: "Some people say Ike would have killed Lewis. . . . That remains to be seen. He wasn't killing me; we were in an even fight when I got caught. He also fought Tua and a lot of people thought Tua won that fight. So how all of a sudden is he going to dominate Lewis? Everybody I talk to thinks he would have been the king. But we will never know. Stacking it all up, I don't see it."

In addition to physical tools and discipline in the ring, emotional discipline is also required when it comes to being a great boxer and competing at a high level for a long time. This is where Ibeabuchi falls short, as Kevin Barry pointed out: "In life, as in sports or in business, you have to not just physically be right but you have to be a full package—a mixture of the physical, the emotional, and the mental. It all has to be in tune and, unfortunately for Ike, he didn't have that."

Things get more complex when we consider the extent to which Ibeabuchi engineered his own downfall—and to what extent we should condemn boxing and the handlers who allowed and encouraged him to fight but never demanded that he seek treatment. for his mental health problems. "It's an unfortunate story," Byrd said. "People were trying to make money from Ibeabuchi. They knew he had problems, but nobody was willing to truly help him."

DiBella pointed out that part of the difficulty was that Ibeabuchi was so resistant to helping himself. "Are there lessons to be taken? Yeah—if you're mentally ill you need to understand that it is an illness and that you have an opportunity to be treated to recover and get better. So you have to try to do something about it. I have empathy for Ike to an extent, because of my belief that he had mental illness. But you can't make someone get help if they don't admit they need it."

Cedric Kushner is no longer here to defend himself—he died in 2015—but his apparent failure to insist that Ibeabuchi get help remains morally questionable. "Up until the final arrest in Las Vegas, Cedric had no doubts [about working with Ike]," said Greg Juckett. "I think he realized he had this incredible asset. He realized how good this guy really was and I think Cedric was willing to go through anything and try anything to keep him and get him a shot at the title."

Eric Bottjer admitted he was deeply uncomfortable with how Ibeabuchi's career played out, and boxing's complicity in his fall. "I don't think anything bad of Ike Ibeabuchi. He can't help the fact that he's mentally ill. I don't know if he can help being violent or not—that's another question. But one of the things about his story that is so tragic is that because he was a world-class boxer and because he had the potential to generate a lot of money nobody tried to help him or protect the people around him that he was capable of hurting. It was simply a case of trying to make his problems go away long enough so he could fight Lennox Lewis and earn a lot of money. Steve Munisteri was a good guy and Cedric was a good guy but I always thought the whole movement to get him out of jail after two violent incidents was wrong. We also need to look at the system here—when you're in prison, does it really improve your state of mind? Nobody came out of this looking good."

Ultimately, everyone around Ibeabuchi—and Ike himself—got so seduced by the allure of the heavyweight championship that they failed to see the human tragedy happening in front of them. The tragedy of a talented but troubled man who needed help but never received it.

Yet the dream that moved Ibeabuchi to travel from Nigeria to America in search of boxing glory remains a seductive one.

Jim Lampley has watched many such dreams live and die during his years in boxing. "Everybody in the sport—whether you're Cedric Kushner, Lou DiBella, or Curtis Cokes—has the dream to get hold of somebody who might have some conceivable shot at becoming the heavyweight champion," he said. "If you can get that championship, it takes your life to the next level. Ibeabuchi was a dream commodity for everyone involved with him."

All of which takes us back to Texas, where Ibeabuchi originally learned his trade, and his dream—for a time—looked like it might really come true. Many believe that Cokes, who died in May 2020 at the age of eighty-two, always carried the disappointment of Ibeabuchi's self-destruction with him. Days after attending Cokes's funeral, Richard Lord recalled: "Curtis didn't talk about [Ibeabuchi] much. He'd just shake his head in disgust. He kinda watched it all happen. And it broke his heart."

Bob Spagnola was another who got caught up in the dream, as he freely admits. Perhaps a little part of him still is. "It was a helluva ride. A helluva story," he said. "One minute Ike was sitting there making $3,500 or $4,500 fighting eight-rounders, then all of a sudden he beats Tua and we started to believe. . . . But then every fighter you're with [causes you to] dream. You think this is gonna be the guy, he's gonna be different, we're gonna do it right, he's gonna get his chance and he'll always love and respect us for what we've done. . . ."

You can still hear the dream in Ike Ibeabuchi's voice as he talks about coming back and winning the title.

You can see it in the desperate legal appeals he files to free himself from custody and chase the dream all over again.

For Ike Ibeabuchi the dream will never come true.

But it won't die either.

T hank you to the following for graciously sharing their memories and thoughts: Claude Abrams, Kevin Barry, Bill Benton, Eric Bottjer, Chris Byrd, Bob Canobbio, Lou DiBella, Tris Dixon, Gary Edwards, Ismael Garcia, Graham Houston, Kirk Johnson, Greg Juckett, Jim Lampley, Richard Lord, Mike Marley, Larry Merchant, Steve Munisteri, Dr. Kafayah Ogunsola, Greg Pickrom, Tim Ray, Bob Spagnola, Ron Scott Stevens, Bruce Trampler, and Mitch Winston.

Although this book is not sanctioned by Ike Ibeabuchi or his family, I must thank Mr. Ibeabuchi for agreeing to an interview in 2016, as well as his half-brother Stan and John Wilkinson for facilitating it. Others whose help in setting up interviews, who deserve thanks are Russ Anber, Eric Bottjer, Greg Juckett, Jack Reiss, Bob Spagnola, Sean Sullivan, and Michael Taylor.

For invaluable advice, encouragement, and support, I must thank Graham Houston, Mark Butcher, Paul Zanon, Luca Rosi, A. J. Rodriguez, and all the team at the late and lamented *Boxing Monthly* magazine and website. A special thanks to Luca, Paul, and A. J. for invaluable editorial feedback and advice. Thanks also to Don McRae for support and encouragement and to Kyle and Andy at Hamilcar.

Above all, thanks to my family and friends, particularly my wife and children, whose love nourishes and sustains me.

SOURCES

Books

Things Fall Apart by Chinua Achebe; *Path to Nigerian Freedom* by Obafemi Awolowo, *Kid Lightning and the Wave of Peace (Right Back)* by Mitch Winston

Newspapers

Austin American-Statesman, Boston Globe, The Californian, Dayton Daily News, Detroit Free Press, Fort Worth Star-Telegram, Herald News, Kokomo Tribune, Las Vegas Review-Journal, Las Vegas Sun, Los Angeles Times, Marshfield News Herald, Montana Standard, New York Daily News, New York Times, Nigerian Spokesman, North County Times, Pacific Daily News, Pensacola News, Philadelphia Daily News, Reno Gazette, Sacramento Bee, Shreveport Times, Tahoe Daily Tribune, Tampa Bay Times, Times Herald, Town Talk, South Florida Sun Sentinel, Vancouver Sun.

Magazines

Boxing Monthly, Boxing News, KO, Professional Boxing Update, The Ring

Websites

azbn.gov, beta.compuboxdata.com, boxingmonthly.com, boxingscene .com, clarkcounty.nv.gov, corrections.az.gov, ESPN.com, fromthevault .hbo.com, helpikeibeabuchi.org, Ice.gov, judicialrecords.wilco.org, nvcourts.gov, nyfights.com, sherdog.com, sports.yahoo.com, superiorcourt.maricopa.gov, usmarshals.gov, washoesheriff.com

ABOUT THE AUTHOR

Luke G. Williams has been a journalist and writer for twenty years. A former staff writer for uefa.com, sportal.com, and euro2000.com, his freelance work has been published in *The Guardian*, *The Independent*, *The Sunday Express*, and *007* magazine. Williams's book *Richmond Unchained* was published to widespread acclaim in 2015, and he was a feature writer and online editor of *Boxing Monthly* magazine. He is now a regular contributor to the website Boxing Social and currently lives in South London.

President of Pandemonium is set in 9.5-point Palatino, which was designed by Hermann Zapf and released initially in 1949 by the Stempel foundry and later by other companies, most notably the Mergenthaler Linotype Company. Named after the sixteenth-century Italian master of calligraphy Giovanni Battista Palatino, Palatino is based on the humanist typefaces of the Italian Renaissance, and reflects Zapf's expertise as a calligrapher. The book was designed by Brad Norr Design, Minneapolis, Minnesota, and typeset by New Best-set Typesetters Ltd.

READ A
SAMPLE CHAPTER
FROM
BERSERK

Birth of a Nightmare

Few things are sadder than the truly monstrous.
—Nathanael West, *The Day of the Locust.*

During the early morning hours of Sunday, April 18, 2010, in the lobby of a hotel in Valencia, Carabobo, one of the best fighters Venezuela had ever produced spoke quietly with his wife. He was a celebrity in his country, a fiercely patriotic man, a proud father of two. Though the couple presented a relaxed picture, the poor woman was probably shaking with worry. Edwin Valero, twenty-eight, had for weeks seemed hell-bent on killing her.

The hotel staff may have sensed that Valero's circuitry wasn't quite right, and hadn't been for a long time. The feelings of paranoia that had jabbed at him in recent times were now wading in with more withering volleys: the suspicion that his wife was having an affair; the fear that people meant to do him harm; and the fear that police, gangsters, even his own mother were conspiring against him.

Ugly stories seeped out of Venezuela. Valero was unhinged and out of control. He'd spent nine days in psychiatric care. His wife had been hospitalized with mysterious injuries. Yet his manager was still trying to set up a fight for him in Mexico. Valero hadn't yet fought a major opponent, but pundits had dubbed him the sport's next moneymaker. He was the fantasy of all boxing fans, a reformed street fighter with a sledgehammer punch who didn't even need proper leverage to knock opponents cold.

"He loved to be in the ring," said Rudy Hernandez, a trainer who knew Valero in earlier days. "I told him, 'The difference between you and a lot of other fighters here is that you love being in the ring. That's why you're going to be a superstar. Keep working as hard as you do, and you'll be the next superstar of boxing.'"

He'd come at opponents like an evil spirit. He was a bizarre vision of a fighter: he'd charge in with his hands low, his eyes ablaze with cold fire. Sometimes he'd yell or hiss when he threw punches. To be in the ring with him must have been nightmarish. "There is something inside me that I have to unleash on someone," Valero once said. "Perhaps it's anger, hatred I feel at having been denied a childhood."

Gales of paranoia whipped through his mind now. Increasingly distrustful and depressed, Valero had spent the weeks after his latest victory arguing with family members and embarrassing himself in public. He believed criminals from Venezuela's underworld were following him. He confessed to a doctor that he was a drug addict. He told his manager that events in his childhood haunted him.

He was in a morbid tailspin. A psychologist said Valero's problems stemmed from an old head injury and extended drug use. The word "psychotropic" appeared repeatedly in medical reports.

Just two months earlier he'd scored an impressive tenth-round stoppage of Antonio DeMarco, a solid fighter who some had predicted would stand up to Valero. In the early rounds, DeMarco boxed well. Yet Valero grew stronger with each passing round, roaring forward like the living bulldozer in Theodore Sturgeon's old science fiction tale, *Killdozer*. DeMarco's corner, realizing their man was done, stopped the fight after the ninth. It was the greatest victory of Valero's career, but after this bout his strange behavior reached a scary crescendo.

The fighter's wife, Jennifer, had dealt with his behavior for years. For reasons known only to other women who endure abusive husbands, she stayed with him. Perhaps it was for the sake of their two children, eight-year-old Edwin Jr. and five-year-old Jennifer Roselyn. Valero loved his children. He had been abandoned by his own father and vowed to give his son and daughter the love he hadn't been given. But bizarre things happened around the Valero home. He once took Jennifer to the hospital with a bullet wound in her left leg. He said gangsters had driven by their home in Caracas and shot her. Meanwhile, he had his chest tattooed with the face of Venezuela's president Hugo Chávez and played around with unregistered guns.

As the clock reached 1:35 a.m., Edwin and Jennifer made their way to room 624. Valero had asked the staff to check under the bed to make sure no one was hiding there. He believed someone had been following him and Jennifer all night. Once he was satisfied the room was empty, he and Jennifer went inside. There's no telling what went on during the next few hours, or where his paranoia took him, but in that room something terrible happened. At 5:30 a.m. Valero appeared in the lobby. As calmly as one might order something from room service, he told the staff that he had just killed his wife.

• • •

He was a storyteller.

He described his early days as if he'd been born in the Seventh Circle of Hell. People absorbed the stories and spewed them out in different ways. Some said he'd been a homeless child, starving in the street. Others said he was an industrious little kid who went door to door selling bags of garlic to housewives. You get the sense that he had some unimaginably hard times but manufactured a frightening autobiography to amuse people. He was selling uplift and desperation.

We know his father left the family. Edwin mentioned it in practically every interview. The father, Antonio Domingo, eventually got sick of being the villain in his son's story.

"Ask my other children if I have been a bad father," he said. "I left the house because of problems with his mother, but I never abandoned them, I was always aware and I helped them financially. Edwin told me one day: 'Dad, I say all that because it gives me more fame, so they see me as the child who suffered a lot.'"

Domingo asked Valero to stop telling those stories. Valero never stopped. Valero controlled the narrative. He was hawking poor pitiful me.

Yet, even if he enjoyed portraying himself as the forsaken child who fought his way out of the rubble of Venezuela, other family members say Valero's childhood was indeed traumatizing for him. He cried often, even as an adult. He was stuck on the idea that he'd been deprived of a regular upbringing. "Edwin had a void that he never explained," said his younger brother Luis. "He never said what he felt."

Listen to his family and friends. You might find yourself believing he never touched drugs until the months before he killed Jennifer. Listen to them. You might even believe he didn't kill her. You might end up believing the stories about kidnappers and thugs and government conspiracies.

The trainers and sparring partners who knew Valero won't buy that he had major mental malfunctions. A psychologist who diagnosed Valero in Venezuela dropped a word: *schizophrenia*. Valero's old gym acquaintances can't accept such things. He'd been too focused. He could hit a heavy bag so hard that the foundation of the city seemed to quake. How could such a good fighter be schizophrenic? Old-time head doctors had a term for it: *funneling*. A person like Valero could focus on something with a sniper's precision even as his mind frayed at the edges. It's that ability to focus that kept the bad thoughts at bay. Of course, this kind of focus only works for a while. The mind falls in on itself.

Jennifer was no match for him. Valero once told a reporter he wished he could keep his wife and children in a crystal box so no harm could come to them. When she was found dead, the blood from her slit throat had clotted on the hotel carpet. It looked like a small pig had been slaughtered. Still, her body was placed on the floor very much like a little doll in a box.

Some reports said he had taken her to the hotel against her will. Others said they were both on the way to a rehab center in Cuba. She was a drug user. She needed help too. The story has two sides. And with each side, there are those who deny and debate and disbelieve.

You could tell it as a straight psycho tale. You could simply focus on her injuries. The bite marks. The gunshot wound. The perforated lung. The time she overdosed and nearly fell off the roof of their apartment. The sad look on her face as she sat ringside. He's winning championships. She's fearing for her life.

You could tell it that way. You could get away with it. There's a thirst for madness. You could draw from a big pool of nasty details and rumors.

He had secrets. We learned enough of them to think we knew him. We'll never know him.

The Venezuelan media treated the Valero case as a tragedy. The American coverage made it a horror story. It's possible that it was both. You take what you need and project it to your audience. Americans like to judge; Venezuelans wanted a hero.

He's dead now. Mental illness and drug addiction took him down. He was found in a jail cell, a picture of his family stuffed into his mouth.

He's dead now.

He doesn't care how the story is told.

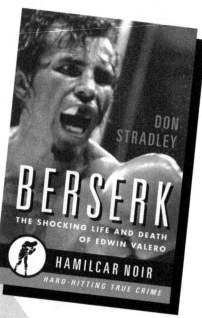

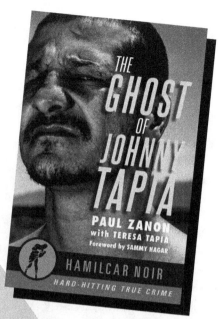

ALSO READ

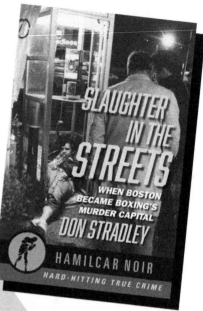

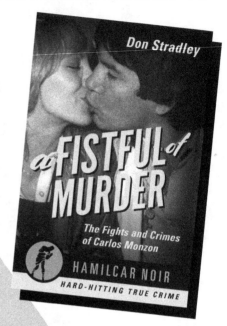

BORN FROM A BOXING MIND

Established in 2003, Rival Boxing Gear has since become a global leader in the industry, with some of the best fighters in the world having entrusted their hands to us. The RFX-Guerrero Pro Fight Glove has been used by some of boxing's greatest champions in World Title fights.

9 781949 590357